VERY GOD

an artist explores the Nicene Creed

OTHER BOOKS BY
CHRIST JOHN OTTO

An Army Arising:
Why Artists are on the Frontline of the Next Move of God

Body
Where You Belong
Red Book of Poetic Theology for Artists

Bezalel
Image of God
Yellow Book of Poetic Theology for Artists

Mary
Honor and Value
Blue Book of Poetic Theology for Artists

Drip

VERY GOD

an artist explores the Nicene Creed

CHRIST JOHN OTTO

Belonging House Media

Very God:
An Artist Explores the Nicene Creed.
by Christ John Otto, Manchester, New Hampshire, USA.
Copyright © 2022 Belonging House Media, LLC.
Revised October 2022.

ISBN: 978-1-7360346-9-9

Library of Congress Control Number: 2022912441

CONTENTS

THE NICENE CREED

Once a week
over one billion human beings
stand up
and recite
a work of theology
and poetry.

They are stating the core beliefs
of the Christian faith.

This weekly pledge of allegiance to
the Holy Trinity
has been going on for almost 1600 years.

The book you are reading began with a series of talks
given on Sundays to the Belonging House community.
We call this group "Beth Charashim."
In English, "the House of Artisans."

This walk through the Creed is unhurried,
and I have taken the time to stop
and unpack important ideas
and also write from an unusual point of view.

I am an artist, and I speak to artists.
My desire is to see a million creative professionals
become disciples of Jesus Christ.
In fact, we pray for a
sanctified,
fearless
body of mature disciples
who rebuild and restore culture.
My hope is that when you read this explanation of the Creed
you too will want to be a disciple of Jesus.

This book is written to people who may not
really care about the theological arguments
that religious people have with the creed.

I am interested in answering questions
that people really ask me
as I sit in coffee shops and ride on trains
all over the world.

This isn't an academic book.
There aren't any footnotes,
and very few references.
If you know your Bible,
you will recognize that
there is a lot of Bible in this book
but I have chosen to refer to the text
the same way the early church fathers did
in their writings.
In other words,
this book doesn't use
the Bible to prove
any arguments,
but is rather formed and shaped by the Bible.

Around the year 250 A.D.
a demographic shift happened in the Roman Empire.
A "tipping point" happened regarding Christianity,
and huge numbers of new believers
came into the church.
This new influx of Christians
came from all walks of life,
not just the lower classes
or from the outer provinces of the Empire.
From what we can tell,
this period may be one of the first instances
of a revival or renewal in the church.

In the second half of the third century (A.D. 250-300)
there was growing pressure
from an increasingly activist
imperial government
to make Christians submit

to what were known as "Roman Values:"
sacrificing to the gods,
participating in public festivals,
and joining in the worship of the emperor.

Under pressure from his advisors,
the Emperor Diocletian
consulted the Oracle of Apollo
about whether or not to eradicate the Christians.
Under direction from the Oracle,
the Great Persecution of Diocletian began in 303.
The Oracle of Apollo
was dedicated to the worship of the sun god, Apollo.

From 303-313 the Great Persecution raged.
Very few churches had property,
but those that did saw that property
seized or destroyed.
Clergy were publicly
and brutally
tortured
and executed.
All church funds
were seized
and Christians
were hunted down
by state sanctioned mobs.

The Roman population eventually lost the taste for persecution
with the martyrdom of St. Agnes,
a twelve year old girl.
People began to see persecution for what it was,
the senseless murder of innocent and upright people.
Even so, the official position was not changed.

In 312,
at the Battle of the Milvian Bridge,
Constantine saw a sign in the sky.

It was a cross over the sun,
and the Chi-Rho monogram of Christ.
The Chi-Rho to our eyes looks like a "P" over an "X."
You may have seen this sign on churches.
Constantine did not understand the sign,
but the next night,
Jesus appeared to him in a dream and told him
"By this sign you shall conquer."

Constantine put the Chi-Rho
on all the shields of the soldiers
(most of whom were already Christians)
and won the battle.

Constantine became the emperor
of the Western Roman Empire.
At the time,
the Roman Empire was divided
between more than one emperor.
In 313 he issued the Edict of Milan,
making Christianity an officially
recognized
and tolerated religion.

It is out of this furnace of persecution
that in 325 the first Council of Nicea was convened,
and the first version of the Nicene Creed was forged.

In the previous century the church had lost the way.
There were all kinds of teaching floating around,
and the big question was
"Who is Jesus, really?"

A majority of Christians believed the teachings of Arius,
that Jesus was a man who became God after he was enlightened.

The persecution was a living memory
to everyone present at the council.

Most of the bishops had been tortured or imprisoned.
We know that St. Nicholas experienced both.
Many of them bore the physical and psychological scars.
It was out of this trauma
that what we call "orthodox" Christianity
was born.

There are some who claim that Constantine
used the council to inject paganism into the church
and created a syncretistic "catholic" church.
Given the facts of history,
this is highly unlikely.
These men suffered in the name of pagan sun worship,
so it is unlikely they would have allowed this into the church.

The final form of the Creed that we have today
was the product of several more councils,
but the core was forged in 325.

Over the centuries,
it has been translated from the original Greek
into Latin
and then to many languages.

For this book I will be using the version
in the 1979 Book of Common Prayer
used by the Episcopal Church at that time.
It is the version I learned when I was young
and is a more accessible English translation than the one
recently approved by the Roman Catholic Church.
I will attempt to clarify
the places where there are issues with the English translation.

Thanks for joining me on this adventure through
one of the most important documents ever crafted by humanity.

6

We believe in one God,
  the Father, the Almighty,
  maker of heaven and earth,
  of all that is, seen and unseen.

We believe in one Lord, Jesus Christ,
  the only Son of God,
  eternally begotten of the Father,
  God from God, Light from Light,
  true God from true God,
  begotten, not made,
  of one Being with the Father.
  Through him all things were made.
  For us and for our salvation
  he came down from heaven:
  by the Holy Spirit
  he became incarnate from the Virgin Mary,
  and was made man.
  For our sake he was crucified under Pontius Pilate;
  he suffered death and was buried.
  On the third day he rose again
  in accordance with the Scriptures;
  he ascended into heaven
  and is seated at the right hand of the Father.
  He will come again in glory to judge the living and the dead,
  and his kingdom will have no end.

We believe in the Holy Spirit, the Lord, the giver of life,
  who proceeds from the Father and the Son.
  With the Father and the Son he is worshiped and glorified.
  He has spoken through the Prophets.
  We believe in one holy catholic and apostolic Church.
  We acknowledge one baptism for the forgiveness of sins.
  We look for the resurrection of the dead,
  and the life of the world to come. Amen.

We BELIEVE in ONE GOD

The word "Creed"
comes from the first word
of this statement when it was translated into latin: Credo.
The original writers called it the Symbol.
It is a symbol,
a representation,
of what the Kingdom holds to be true.

In this sense,
the Creed is like the American Declaration of Independence:
"We hold these truths to be self evident,
that all men are created equal
and endowed by their creator
with certain inalienable rights."

We believe in One God.
Words are merely symbols
of the reality behind them.

The first word in the Greek is this: pisteuo.
I believe.
It is one of the most important words in the New Testament,
and it occurs 244 times.

Pisteuo is the word that Jesus uses
with the father of the sick child,
"Do you believe?"
And the father replies "Lord, I believe, help my unbelief."

And probably the most important use
of this word is in Romans 10:9
when Paul instructs Jews in Rome that
"If you confess with your mouth Jesus is Lord,
and believe in your heart God raised him from the dead,
you will be saved."

To the Christian of the first millennium,
belief was not a private matter.

To them, what you believe is who you are.
And it is true.
What you believe is what you do.
During the Protestant era,
because everybody had their own version of belief,
we believed that your beliefs were private.
I believe whatever I want,
but I don't share it with anyone else.

In our day,
things are much closer to the world of the Roman Empire.

During the Roman Empire,
for a Christian to stand up,
in a public gathering every Sunday
in a world that worships all kinds of things
gods,
philosophers,
body parts,
cults,
demons,
and emperors,
and say "We believe in one God" is very radical.

And honestly,
we live in a world where people worship all kinds of things,
gods,
philosophers,
entertainment franchises,
body parts,
cults,
demons,
and political parties.
Standing up and doing this is once again radical.

Belief in the Christian context,
in the same way it is for a Jew,
is always the moment to "stand and be counted."

Are you on the Lord's side, or someone else's?
As Joshua asked the angel
"Are you on their side or ours?" (Joshua 5:13)
And the Angel said
"I am neither, I am on the Lord's side."

I promise you this,
all the things you think are important right now—
political parties,
celebrities,
whatever the news is about this week,
plague,
wars,
nations,
races,
and anything else—
all of these are temporary,
and a lot of your concern
about these things in the big arc of history
is rather small.

It should be a reminder to us all
that many have died for standing and saying these words.

50 years after Constantine another emperor arose,
and there was another persecution,
and many gave up their lives
because they would not renounce their faith in Jesus
expressed in the Creed.

When the Vikings rampaged through Britain,
it was this Creed that monks and priests and believers
refused to renounce.
This Creed was the Creed that Mohammed
told believers to renounce at sword-point.
This Creed was on the lips of the martyrs of Japan,
and the first Jesuit missionaries to the New World
who died here at the hands of the Iroquois.

It was this Creed that was on the lips
of most of the 100 million victims of Communism
in the past one hundred years.
This we believe.

And we do not profess belief
in any one
teacher,
or sect,
or denomination.
Paul said in the first chapter of 1 Corinthians
that the believers of that church were into personalities.
"I follow Cephas, and I follow Apollos."
And Paul said he follows Christ.
There is only one rabbi, the Messiah.
There is only one God.

And this One God is the Jewish One God.
He is not one of the Roman pantheon
that has become pre-eminent.
He is not the god of the philosophers,
that is abstract and impersonal.
He is not the flat, one dimensional Allah.
He is YHWH,
I AM,
Hashem,
the Name,
Adonai,
the God of the Bible,
revealed to the prophets.

We believe in the God who is only knowable
when He chooses to reveal himself.
The knowledge we have is not created
by human beings out of our imaginations.
And because of this,
we do not have the right
or the liberty

to redefine,
reimagine,
or remake this God in our own image.
To do this is a work of blasphemy.
This is why the making of idols
in our image is linked
to the worship of other Gods in the first commandment.

What we know about Him comes from Him,
and this knowledge has been given to us
through the witness of those who received the revelation.
That witness to the revelation is in the Bible.

And it follows that the first section of the Creed,
and the first line should come
from the greatest source of revelation
in the Old Covenant:
Moses.

The first line of the Creed is from Deuteronomy 6:4.
"Hear O Israel, the Lord our God is one Lord."
This word is mysterious,
because Moses does not use the number "one" here.
He uses the word "echad."
This is the word for "one" in the sense of a bunch of grapes.
It is one with a plural sense.
One "Whole."
And Jesus continues this idea in John 17.
He prayed that we would be brought into this "Oneness."
This is "Wholeness."
So right here, we see that the oneness of God
is mysterious and encompasses much more than a singularity.

And when we stand and say "yes" to this truth,
we are forsaking all others.
There are no other Gods,
and to give our attention to any other thing is an illusion.

This is why,
when Paul discussed the eating of food dedicated to idols,
he said it was a sign of weakness to make it an issue.
When you are fully aware of the bigness of God,
the completeness,
the wholeness,
the supremacy,
and the glory of God,
you see that all other things
are either
an illusion
or a distraction.
One God.
Over all.

We believe in One God.

the FATHER
the ALMIGHTY

About 20 years ago I attended a men's conference.
The speaker asked everyone to stand up.
There were about 200 men in the room.
Then he asked everyone
who did not know
who their father was
to sit down.

About 20 men sat down.

Then he asked everyone in the room
who did not know
who their father's father was
to sit down.

About half that were standing sat down.

And then he asked everyone
who did not know
who their father's father's father was
to sit down.

There were only two men standing.

The disconnection with father
is one of the deepest places
of brokenness
in the Western world.
It is a tender spot for nearly everyone I meet.
For many,
their "father wound"
defines their entire existence.

The worst thing
Jesus ever said
to his accusers was in Matthew 22:29:
"You know not the Scriptures,
nor the power of God."

And sadly, when you are broken,
you do not know you can be healed,
and so you make your brokenness your reality.
And then we create systems
and solutions based on our reality
and force it onto others.

One of the saddest things about our age
is that we let people
who know not the Scriptures nor the power of God
dictate to us what we believe,
how we should believe,
and how we can talk about what we believe.

And sadly,
many in the church have accepted
the foolish idea
that becoming culturally relevant
will make us more accessible to unbelievers.

In other words,
becoming like the culture around us
will be an effective means of evangelism.

It doesn't work because the culture is broken.

And so,
many Christians pull back
from the notion that God is Father,
because fatherhood and male authority
is seen as a form of
"toxic masculinity."

Our calling is not to become like the broken,
but to heal the brokenhearted.
To set the captive free,
and to proclaim the Lord's favor
in the lives of the hurting.

And in our day,
we have to embrace a firm position about some things.
This really is "tough love."

As I said in the last chapter,
our faith is a revealed religion.
In other words,
everything we know about God
we have received from God,
by God.

God has told us who He is,
what He is like
and how we should understand Him.
And Jesus said in John 14:9
that He was the highest form of this revelation,
and that if we have seen Him
we have seen the Father.

God is Father.
And Paul tells us in Romans 8:1-17
that if we have received Jesus,
are baptized and filled with the Holy Spirit,
we will be adopted by this Father,
we will become a joint heir with Jesus,
a member of this God family,
and by the power of the Holy Spirit
we ourselves will cry "Abba, Father."

That is the most intimate form
of the word for "father" in Hebrew,
and it is still used
both in Hebrew and Arabic as the word for father.
It is the first word most Israeli babies say.

So from Jesus, our rabbi,
the Messiah,
we must affirm that God is Father.

There are lots of implications to this,
but the first and most important is this:
God is the Most Relational Being in the Universe.

The first word used to describe God
in the Creed is relational and organic.
Probably the greatest mistake
the church made in history
was to use abstract philosophical terms
to describe and understand God,
and forget that Biblical terms are concrete and relational.

When I started seminary,
the first class did not begin with the Bible,
it began with Socrates and Plato:
God is immutable,
omnipresent,
omniscient,
transcendent,
and omnipotent.
God is
the true,
the good,
and the beautiful.

Wisely,
the Creed does not
begin there.
God is personal,
not a force,
a vague unmoved mover,
not the good, the true, and the beautiful.
Although these impersonal descriptions contain truth.

No.
God is your organic source,
you bear a genetic resemblance to Him at a profound level.
God is by nature concerned about your welfare.

God is concerned for your protection,
your provision,
your success,
your inheritance,
and his legacy through you.

You are the image of your Father,
at so deep and profound a level,
that even in the fallenness and brokenness
of this distorted world,
God is concerned about redeeming and rescuing you.

This is why the Reformed concept
of total depravity is in error.
It makes the point too strong.

You, even on your worst day,
still bear the image of God.
This is why unbelievers
and cultures that have never heard the gospel
can create art and stories
that reflect deep truth and concepts
that reflect the Kingdom.

There is a deep collective memory
of Truth in your being.

All creation bears the fingerprints of the Father.
This God is the Father of the Prodigal Son in Luke,
who is willing to give up half his possessions
and then longingly waits for the fool to return,
after he has squandered his wealth
on sex, drugs, and rock n' roll.
This Father,
on seeing his son,
runs to him and gives him his robe,
his ring,
and kills the fatted calf.

One key revelation is this word from Jesus,
from John 14:
If you have seen me
you have seen the Father.

And Jesus said in John 5:19
that He only does what He sees the Father doing.

And if we look at Jesus,
we learn two things.
First we learn a lot about the Father in Heaven:

Jesus Christ went about doing good,
healing all those who were tormented by the devil. (Acts 10:38)

When He saw the multitudes, He had compassion on them
for they were like sheep without a shepherd. (Matthew 9:36)

Suffer the little children to come unto me
for to such as these belongs the Kingdom of Heaven.
(Matthew 19:14)

Come unto me all you who are weary and heavy laden,
and I will give you rest,
take my yoke upon you and learn of me,
for my yoke is easy and my burden is light. (Matthew 11:28)

Woman, where are your accusers?
Neither do I accuse you.
Go and sin no more. (John 8:10)

If you have seen me,
you have seen the Father.

Second,
we learn a lot about God's intention for fatherhood.
What the world tells us about fatherhood is a lie.

It is amazing if you watch a lot of
television, movies, and now streaming shows,
how every plot tells you
the father is
not smart,
very lazy--or works at a job that is a mystery,
and is looking for the next opportunity
to commit adultery and drink beer.
Here and there you get Ward Cleever
from the American television show
Leave it to Beaver,
the dad who is absent most of the time
but then speaks some
platitude that fixes everything
at the end of the 20 minute story.

The culture tells us a father is either
a buffoon, or a cold distant fixer.
We cannot project
these lies from the world, the flesh, and the devil
back onto God.

And likewise we cannot make theology
based in our disappointments, hurts, pain, or abuse.

Both of these tendencies are forms of idolatry:
making a god in our own image.

This is why language,
and how we talk about God,
for both the Jew and the Christian,
is so important.
God revealed himself to us through language,
and Scripture tells us that one day
we will have to answer for every stray word we utter.

We cannot submit to language dictated to us by unbelievers—
who know not the Scriptures nor the power of God.

God is not female.
I do get emails about this periodically,
and it comes from a misunderstanding
of gender pronouns in ancient languages.
English does not have genders for nouns like French.
In French a table uses the feminine article.
It is a feminine noun.
That does not mean tables have ladyparts.
It is a convention of that language.
In the ancient languages the word for "spirit" *ruach*
is a feminine noun in Hebrew
and *pneuma*, neuter in Greek.
Throughout history this has been a problem
because we have no neuter in English.
Many Christians have a vague belief in the Holy Spirit
because the King James Bible translated *spirit* "it."

There is also a misunderstanding
of the concepts of the masculine and feminine.

In all honesty,
since the 1970's
Western culture has suffered from gender confusion.

Yes,
Adam and Eve together reflect the image of God,
but that does not mean that God
is some sort of hermaphrodite being.
It means that the true Masculine force of God—
directive and initiating,
is mysteriously wed to the Feminine force—
receptive, and responsive.
Somehow in the mystery of the Holy Trinity
there is both Initiation and Reception.
It is a dance,
and we will never understand it,
just as in human relationships
the dance

between men and women
is mysterious.

Recently a friend said that they believed
the Holy Spirit was female
and that she referred to the Holy Spirit
by a female name she created.
It is God's business to sort people out,
but honestly, this is a grave error.
So for the record,
I refer to God as He.
Fathers are "he's" not "she's."
It is really sad that we have to re-state realities
in a world gone mad.
But honestly,
it is this madness that the Christian is always called to correct.
The Roman world was mad in this area as well,
and it was the clarity of the Gospel
that changed all that.

The blood of the martyrs bought the sanity of civilization.

I have lots of experience
working in religious settings that
mandated
verbal gymnastics
to avoid referring to God as "he."
When you play with language
you distort the concept of how you understand God.

Language is a symbol for how you think
and how you organize reality.

Distorted language will create a distorted reality.
The personal,
relational,
good Father becomes more and more vague,
and you lose the way.

Then you have the Father-Mother God,
then you start calling God female names,
and then you start making up gods in your own image.
And very quickly you move into
paganism,
the occult,
witchcraft,
and sexual perversion.
I am an eyewitness to this descent into evil
in the clergy I worked with.
It happened right before my eyes in the Episcopal Church
and the United Methodist Church.
It began in the church in the 1990's, while I was in seminary.
There is a slippery slope.

Language matters,
because this is essential to the nature of our Father.

There is an old joke
about a boy who comes home from school,
and tells his mother he got a part in the play.
His mother asks, "What kind of part did you get?'
The boy replied, "I play the father."
The mother, visibly upset responds:
"You go right back to school
and tell that teacher you want a speaking part!"

Our God is not that kind of Father.
Our Father is always speaking.

Our God speaks,
and through His voice
guides,
directs,
heals,
reveals,
and in the voice of the Father,
we somehow find ourselves.

The Father, as all fathers were created to do,
creates and defines our identity.

And right here,
you can see one of the key strategies
of satan against fathers.
If you destroy the father,
the child does not know who they are.
And when the father is absent,
the child never breaks free from the mother.
And so for life,
the child never stands up on their own,
never leaves the nest,
and expects to be a giant coddled baby for life.
It is the voice of the Father
that calls us out,
and breaks us free,
to become fully who we are meant to be.

And this leads to the second description of his nature.
Almighty.

The power of God is in his voice.
And that voice is Almighty.
That voice, as Psalm 29 tells us
is more powerful than the waters.

I grew up as a child near Niagara Falls,
and my mother would take me for walks,
and I remember the roar of the water,
and the vibrations.
The ground near the Niagara River shakes.
It powers the two largest power-plants in North America,
sending electricity
to Toronto, Chicago, Cleveland, Buffalo, and New York City.
Our God spoke that into being.
The Bible begins with the voice of God,
and the Bible is the record of the voice of God.

Jesus said in John 10 that his sheep know his voice.
This recognition of the voice of God is another aspect
of our organic relationship to the Father.
We were made by,
respond to,
and are guided and directed by,
this Voice.

And this Almighty power holds all things together
and in order.
All things came to being from this Father.
All things were started by this Father.
All things will be finished by this Father.
And before all things this Father existed,
and after all things are over,
He will be.

He is who He is.
He will be who He will be.
Almighty.
I AM.

This is very Jewish.
Judaism teaches that truth is
two paradoxical concepts held together.

God is Truth,
and Truth is a person.
The intimate Father
who knows and loves you
is also the
ALMIGHTY I AM
ALL POWERFUL.

It is too much for our minds to grasp.
But a Christian cannot separate
the Father from the Almighty.

As one of my mentors
Dr. Robert Tuttle once said,
"All heresy is man's mind trying
to remove the tension of great paradoxes."

The ALMIGHTY GOD without the FATHER is the force,
the universe,
the energy,
the vibe.

And that becomes a nothing.
So abstract that it makes no sense.
It drifts into new age weirdness or Jungian psychology
which always leads us back to
paganism,
the occult,
witchcraft and
sexual perversion.
Interesting.

And the Father who is not Almighty
is Santa Claus.
An amoral,
warm fuzzy,
"love wins"
kind of grandpa in the sky.

"Awe shucks,
kids will be kids,
have a lolly.
Go have fun,
but don't hurt yourself or anybody else."

Jesus forces us to hold all things in tension.
The kind,
intimate,
loving Father
with the One who is full of all power,

who made the universe,
and all that is in it.

If you have seen me,
you have seen the Father.

This is why
we must always
be called back to the center.

God is Spirit,
and they that worship Him
Worship in Spirit and in Truth.

I believe in One God,
the Father,
the Almighty.

MAKER of all things VISIBLE and INVISIBLE

If God is the Almighty Father
then it makes logical sense that God is
Creator.

When you are a Father,
you need to do two things:
give life
and have someone to
guide,
direct,
and provide for.

I tend to recite the creed in the old form
I learned in Sunday School.
The older version of the Creed
in English used the word "Maker."
I prefer "maker"
over "creator" for many reasons,
in part because that term is used in both the Greek and Hebrew.

Being a Maker
is an essential aspect
of the Judeo-Christian God.
This God made the World
as we understand it.

These are not abstracts
like the descriptions of God
from Socrates and Plato.
We do not find omniscience and omnipotence.
This system is grounded in reality and Scripture.

God alone is the Source,
and part of His continuing nature
is that God makes things.

And the first half of this clause is rooted in Genesis 1:1,
"In the beginning God created the heavens and the earth."

God made the sky,
and also the spiritual realm.
God made the earth.

Genesis 1 also tells us
that in the Image of God
he made male and female.
So when male and female come together,
the purpose is to create and give life.
It is for this reason that the church
has always been concerned about
marriage,
family,
and childbearing.

Life is intrinsic in what it means
to be a bearer of the Image of God.

We get into trouble
when we make the Bible
answer questions
that it was not written to answer.
And I think you get into trouble
when you try to make the Bible answer scientific questions.
Believing that God is Creator
is not
an anti-intellectual position.

The fool says in his heart that there is no God.

And as we look at the world around us,
we can see that there are many fools
who are credentialed
but not qualified.

Remember that this Creed
was written by men who had suffered
under a great persecution.

They bore in their bodies the scars of torture and imprisonment.
And many of them were not only spiritual giants
who performed signs, wonders, and miracles,
they were also intellectual giants
who spoke multiple languages,
who studied at the universities of Athens and Alexandria,
and who lived in a world
where there were many ideas and philosophies.

In the end,
the Christian worldview
was far superior
to pagan thought,
and it won
in the world of ideas.

We are not going to delve in to evolution beyond this:
There is no answer in Darwinism.
It assumes
that something existed
before evolution happened.
The second law of thermodynamics
says that all things move from order to disorder.
No one has been able to explain to me
this contradiction
between physics and biology.

Scripture says that God existed
before our physical reality
and caused something to happen,
and that cause was not an impersonal process
out of randomness.

That cause was an expression of His personhood,
and the purpose was for relationship.
God is a Father
and a father desires children,
both to give love and to receive love.

Love,
although not stated,
is deeply assumed in Creation.
Creation is an act of love.

And the Bible also says that after this created order,
there is going to be another incorruptible order.
There is some kind of physical substance that will be
that is beyond our understanding.

Although the Bible tells us creation happened
when God spoke,
the Creed,
for brevity,
does not.

The belief that God is Maker
is very important for artists, and creative professionals,
because although all human beings
are bearers of the image of God,
it is the artist,
artisan,
and creative person
who most clearly reflects this image,
because Maker
is one of the four core descriptions
of who God is.

And this description of creator
is reinforced in the Greek New Testament,
when God is called "an artisan."

Hebrews 11:10 in the Greek
does not say
that God is "architect and builder."

It says that God is the Master Artisan,
and the Demiurge.

Demiurge is a term
that was well known at the time of the New Testament
and is a word used by Plato in his *Republic*
(the only direct reference to Plato in the New Testament).

The Demiurge
was a divine artisan
who fashioned and created the physical universe.

Jesus himself, in the Greek,
was an artisan and the son of Joseph the artisan.
This was the profession God chose when he walked the earth.
To receive the calling
to the arts and to be a maker
is to receive a calling to be like God.
That alone is profound.

Your calling to be an artist
or creative person is
a living parable for the world to see.
You are called
to be a living example of the Christian life
in concrete realities.
I think this is probably the chief reason
there is a constant war for the arts.

So the act of creation is not limited
to the beginning of this world.
Creation is expressed in the call of God.

Cara, the world for "call,"
is used several times in Genesis 1.

God called the light day, and the dark night.
God called the water and the land.
God called it good.
And when God spoke to Abraham,
He called him and created a new nation.

When God spoke to Bezalel,
he called him and created not only the Tabernacle,
but also the whole Jewish symbolic system.

And when Jesus was on the mountain in Mark 3:14,
it says he called the twelve,
and in the Greek he "made" them apostles.
Before that moment
there had never been something like an apostle before.
That word is not translated properly:
usually it reads "appointed" or "ordained."
The original word was not religious.
It was just like in the shop of Joseph
where they "made" things.

Jesus spoke and
made them into apostles.
The call of God and the nature of God
as Maker cannot be separated.
When you hear a call
from God,
you are made into something new.

The Creed takes creation to another level though:
This Creator is the creator of all that is,
seen
and unseen.

All that is:
"Interstellar space and planets in their courses."
Before the telescope.
Cells and bacteria,
Before the microscope.
Electrons,
Protons,
and Quarks,
before Einstein and Quantum Physics.

All that is,
seen and unseen.
The writers of the Creed knew there was more.
They knew that they did not understand everything,
and that human beings would continue to
discover,
invent,
and uncover
the mysteries in our world
forever.

We affirm
every time we say the Creed,
that God is bigger than we are,
the world is bigger than we know,
the galaxies,
the universe,
the dimensions,
and the spiritual realm—
is bigger than we know.
There is always room
in the Christian faith for discovery and the unknown.

There is more,
and we are made in the image
and called
to become like
the one who made all these things
and who understands them all.

So often people who believe
in true
Biblical Christianity
are smug and self-important.
They act like they have all the answers
and know all the answers.
For as big as God and the Kingdom are,
their minds are very small.

Honestly,
if you believe this faith,
your posture needs to be one of awe and wonder.

This One who knows all,
who fills all,
who created all,
(even things we have not yet discovered),
is my Father.
I am his child.
I am made in this Image.
And I am called to be like Adam,
on a journey of discovery and naming.

The calling
of the Christian believer
is to embrace this core truth,
and then embark
on the task of rebuilding a broken earth
and by extension
a broken creation,
seen and unseen.

I believe in one God,
the Father,
the Almighty,
Creator of heaven and earth,
of all that is, seen and unseen.

41

we believe in
ONE LORD
JESUS
CHRIST

The Creed is divided into three sections,
each beginning with the affirmation
We believe.

Before we get too deep in the second part of the Creed,
let's define some terms going forward.

This faith is the "catholic"
and "orthodox" faith.

Catholic means universe or universal.
It comes from a very common Jewish practice:
Baruch atta Adonai, Eloheinu malech ha olam.
"Blessed are you Lord our God, King of the Universe."

The Greek ending of that prayer is "Katholikon."

It is the faith that is true
throughout the universe,
in all times and places.
What all true believers believed in every place at all times.

And what we profess is the Orthodox faith.
That is, the true faith.
This is the revealed faith.
And that word "orthodox" can be understood
more than one way.
It can mean worship or belief.

And this is extremely important:
true faith leads to true worship.

Orthodox can be translated both ways.
The faith we profess is expressed in the worship we give.

In Latin there is an old rule:
"Lex orandi, Lex credendi."
How we pray is how we believe.

I think this is so important to remember,
and why the Creeds have such a different tone
than the many "Statements of Faith"
issued by various denominations and organizations.

As you found in the first section of the Creed,
when you stop and look into it,
it fills you with the majesty of God.
This document is rooted in the all encompassing truth of God,
and is intended to lead one to true worship.
The fullness of the faith is not cerebral.
It is not just an agreement
to a set of precepts and statements.

It is about your life,
your worship,
your prayer,
and your relationship with God and other people.
Ultimately,
it is about not what you think is true,
but your True Identity.

One Lord.
Here the Creed quotes Ephesians 4:5
"One Lord, One Faith, One Baptism."

In the Roman Empire,
the official Roman religion had one Creed:
Caesar o Kurios, Caesar Divi Filius.
Caesar is Lord, Caesar is the Son of God.

And for about one hundred years
the church had only one Creed:
Jesus is Lord.

You can see where the conflict would arise.
This is about the Kingdom,
not about a religion.

And this Kingdom,
as the dream of Nebuchadnezzar revealed in Daniel 3,
would start as a little rock that strikes the Roman Empire:
a mixture of iron and clay,
militarily strong,
but politically weak,
and overtake it.
And this Kingdom would become
the largest of all the Kingdoms
and become a great mountain.
One mountain,
just like the one spoken of in Isaiah 2 and 24.

In a world full of
false messiahs,
false kings,
and false promises
the Creed reminds us of this:
Jesus Christ is the one Lord—
One Head over the Body.
One Mediator between God and Humankind.
One High Priest seated at the right hand of the Father.
One Intercessor before the throne
with wounds in his hands and his side.
One King of the Kingdom,
who is King of kings and Lord of lords.
One Name above every other name.

There are not multiple authorities in our lives.
Jesus Christ is the ultimate authority,
and to get fixated on anything else is a distraction.

Although Bill Johnson has gotten flack for saying this,
the orthodox faith teaches us that
"Jesus Christ is perfect theology."

And now we come to the core section of the Creed.
The heart of the Creed is a man.

And this man is clearly identified:
Jesus Christ.

I have been told on numerous occasions
that this name is anti-Semitic.
And I know people who will not use it,
and refuse to say this Creed for that reason.
So let's first talk about the reason Jesus came,
He came to be the light of the nations
and the glory his people Israel.
As we know from history,
Israel,
for the most part,
did not receive him.

And the Christians over time
caused a lot of suffering for the Jews.
Messianic Jews,
mostly coming out of this history of suffering,
try to make sense out of their faith in the Messiah
in the light of their identity as a persecuted minority.
And sadly,
their Messianic faith gets mixed up
in some Protestant beliefs
and you get the proverbial
baby thrown out with the bathwater.
This has resulted in a few weird teachings
as this growing Messianic community
tries to make sense of it all.

As you have seen,
so far,
as we explore the Creed,
many teachings and conspiracy theories
will begin to evaporate in the light
of careful study.

I found an article that explains the origin of the name Jesus and how it came about without my side commentary:

> The name "Jesus" has a long, long history. The origin of this name is the Hebrew name Yehoshu'a (Latinized as Joshua), which means "Yahweh saves." This Hebrew name is first used Exodus in 17:9 where we are introduced to Yehoshu'a Ben Nun.
>
> When this Hebrew name was transliterated in the Greek Septuagint (2,000 year old Greek translation of the Hebrew Bible) it was written as "Iesous." The Greek alphabet had no "Y" sound, so it used the "I" sound. The Greek alphabet has no consonant "H," or equivalent, so this sound is dropped. The Greek alphabet also had no "Sh" sound, so it used the "S" sound. Then, Greek male names end with "s," so the "s" was added. And this is how Yehoshu'a became Iesous in the Greek.
>
> It is common for names to shift and evolve when transferred from one culture to another. For instance, the German name Ludwig is Louis in France and the Spanish name Juan is John in English speaking countries. The Hebrew name Yehoshu'a, is Yeshu'a (Latinized as Jeshua) in the Aramaic language, such as we see in Ezra 2:2. When this Aramaic name was transliterated in the Greek Septuagint, they used the same method as stated above and it comes out to Iesous, the same as it did for Yehoshu'a.
>
> When we come to the New Testament period we find that the name of the Messiah is Iesous in the Greek New Testament, but we find that it is Yeshu'a in the Aramaic New Testament. When the Greek New Testament was translated into Latin in the 4th Century this name was written as Iesus, an exact match to the Greek that it came from. The Latin letter "I" split into two letters, "I" and "J." Originally this was two different ways of writing the

same letter. So the Iesus became Jesus, but they were both pronounced the same way. Years later, some cultures began using the "I" for the vowel sound and "J" for a "Y" sound. It was not until around 1500 AD that the letter J took on the "dg" sound we are familiar with today.

So, the modern name "Jesus" comes from the Latin Iesus, which comes from the Greek Iesous, which comes from the Aramaic Yeshu'a and the Hebrew Yehoshu'a."

That was by Jeff Banner of the Ancient Hebrew Research Centre (ancient-hebrew.org).

And this name is important.
This is the name given to him by God.
When Mary encounters Gabriel
in the first chapter of Matthew,
he tells her:
"You shall call his name Jesus
for he will save his people from their sins." (Matthew 1:21)

In Aramaic
this would have been a play on words
that is lost in translation.

You will call him Salvation,
for he shall save his people
from their sins.

And so, he is given the most common name in his day.
Joshua:
God saves.
Because people were crying out for salvation
from their foreign occupiers,
the Romans.

And it is this name that healed the man
sitting by the beautiful gate.

It is this name that Peter, James, and John
were forbidden to teach in.
It was for this name that many suffered torture and death.

> Conquering kings their titles take
> From the foes they captive make;
> Jesus, by a nobler deed,
> From the thousands he hath freed.
>
> Yes: none other Name is given
> Unto mortals under heaven,
> Which can make the dead arise,
> And exalt them to the skies.
>
> We would gladly for that Name
> Bear the cross, endure the shame;
> Joyfully for him to die
> Is not death, but victory.
>
> Jesus, who dost condescend
> To be called the sinner's Friend,
> Hear us, as to thee we pray,
> Glorying in thy Name today.

But, there are many people named Jesus.
As I said it was a very common name in the first century,
and so this Jesus is given a surname:
Christ.

And this too should not bother you.
It is a literal translation of the word "Messiah."
And this word actually means to "shine" in Hebrew.
In Greek the word means to "be smeared."
So if you live in a sunny Middle Eastern climate,
and someone smears you with a lot of oil
you are going to be shiny in the sun.
They didn't dribble a little oil on you,
they emptied out a large flask and let it run all over you.

A long time ago we were having a prayer meeting
with the Ten Days of Prayer,
and someone decided she was going to anoint me.
She poured the oil out over my head.
It ran down my face,
into my beard,
and all over my shirt.
I was anointed.

So it was with Jesus.
He is the one on whom the Holy Spirit rested.
He was the one who was set apart,
and who would walk in the Power of the Holy Spirit.

And this is important.
The anointing of the Holy Spirit
is the Messianic Promise.
We come into Messiah
Into Christ
by the Holy Spirit,
and in the power of the Holy Spirit
we are created to walk.

When we do this, we are a new creation,
something new the world has never seen before
people who can do the same things--
and greater things--
than Jesus did
because we are anointed by the Holy Spirit.
In the Kingdom it is all about identity.
And your identity is Christian, anointed.

The name Christian
is not the same as being a Jesus follower.
This is a cheap
and inadequate
sellout
to the culture.

Some of our brothers and sisters
think this is hip and relevant,
but Jesus said terrible things
to those who just wanted to follow him,
and reap the benefits of being in the company of a great rabbi.

"No one looking back is fit to man a plow." (Luke 9:62)

"Go sell all that you have and come follow me." (Luke 18:22)

"Foxes have holes and birds of the air have nests,
but the son of man has nowhere to lay his head." (Luke 9:58)

"Let the dead bury their own dead." Luke (9:60)

There is only one way to follow Jesus,
Embrace his perfect death
and come into life.
And when you make that decision,
you have not accepted some teaching.
You have made a spiritual transaction
your old life is gone,
you have a new life,
and a new identity.
You do not belong
to any nation or group,
sect,
or political party.
You are in Christ.
A new nation,
his body.
And you are recreated
to become a little version of him,
a little anointed one
with the Holy Spirit.
A Christian.
You cheapen this
by calling yourself a "Jesus follower."

There is only one name given for health and salvation:
the strong name of our Lord Jesus Christ.

As Paul says in the second chapter of Philippians:

> Have this mind within you,
> which was in Christ Jesus,
> who,
> though he was in the form of God,
> did not count equality with God a thing to be grasped,
> but emptied himself,
> taking the form of a servant,
> being born in the likeness of men.
> And being found in human form he humbled himself
> and became obedient unto death, even death on a cross.
> Therefore God has highly exalted him
> and bestowed on him the name which is above every
> name,
> that at the name of Jesus every knee should bow,
> in heaven and on earth and under the earth,
> and every tongue confess that Jesus Christ is Lord,
> to the glory of God the Father.
> (Philippians 2:5-11)

Jesus Christ, as C.S. Lewis wrote,
descended far below humanity,
so that when he was raised and ascended,
he would raise us up to be seated with him.

Maybe you have never truly called
on the name of the Lord,
and so today I encourage you
to confess this name.

You may have settled for religious performance,
and have come into agreement with the lie
that you have to do something
to make God happy with you.

God is happy with you.

And as we shall see in the coming chapters,
Jesus has done it all.

Maybe you have come into agreement
with the cheap spirit of this age,
and believed some false things about God,
and about yourself.

If either of these things apply to you,
pray this prayer with me.

Lord Jesus,
I confess that I am a sinner,
and that the only way forward for me is to
confess that you are Lord.
I believe that you are the only Son of God,
and that you died on the cross
and rose again from the dead.
Come into my body, mind, soul, and spirit
with the power of the Holy Spirit,
and make me new.
Lord help me see every area in my life
where I have believed that I need to perform
or do something to make you answer prayer,
change people or situations,
or make you happy.
I acknowledge today that I have believed a lie
that you are not good,
and that I have to do things to please you.
I embrace my true identity in you--
I am anointed.
I am chosen.
I am called.
I bear the image of your son.
I am a member of your royal priesthood.
I am a member of the nation of your kingdom.

And I ask you today
to open my eyes
to the fullness of your kingdom,
and the fullness of your anointing today.
It is in the mighty name of Jesus Christ
King of Kings
and Lord of Lords,
that I pray.
Amen.

The only SON of GOD

Thirty years ago I was sitting in class with Dr. Dennis Kinlaw
and he said something in passing:

"If you think that you can preach a gospel
where Jesus became the Son of God,
then you have no gospel to preach at all."

God is the Most Relational Being in the Universe.
You cannot understand the Kingdom
or the New Covenant without relationship.
And as we have already noted,
Relationship is built into the Godhead.
God is Father,
and God relates to the Son and the Holy Spirit.

And if God is a Father,
then it follows that God has a Son.
And that Son,
from his own words,
is the Son of God.

One of the unexpected consequences of going to seminary,
and preparing for the priesthood
was the numbers of people who felt free to tell me their
theological opinions
and attitudes.
And usually this was their explanation
of why they do not go to church
or practice "organized religion."

These conversations often happened
while I was in the check out line
at the grocery store.

One great rule in life is to never argue with people
in the check out line
at the grocery store.

And over time you begin to discover
that these "great thinkers"
didn't have an original idea in their head.
They just kept repeating
the same
boring
things
over and over.

There is not an original lie in the universe.

And one of these unoriginal ideas
that I heard again and again was
"Jesus is God's son just like we are all God's children."
And if my friend is Jewish,
they might say,
"I am a child of God,
because I am Jewish and God is my Father,
and I don't need Jesus."

John 20:31 tells us that his Gospel was written so that
"You may believe
that Jesus is the Messiah, the Christ,
and that you will believe he is the Son of God."

In fact, John's Gospel
continually comes back to the central idea
that Jesus states in John 14.
"If you have seen me,
you have seen the Father."

"I and the Father are one." (John 10:30)

"I only do what I see the Father doing." (John 5:19)

And twice in the life of Jesus
at his baptism, and at the Transfiguration,
the Voice of the Father is heard saying:

"This is my Beloved Son, in whom I am well pleased"

"Listen to him."

I don't know one person in a check out line at the grocery store
that has heard a voice come out of a cloud,
and say that about them.

There is a continual onslaught on this one phrase,
because it is the central reality of the Gospel.
We are coming to the heart of the matter:
God became a Man.

There is another religion that
several times each day
stops and proclaims that God has no son,
and puts those words on their buildings.
There is a group of intellectuals called the Jesus Seminar
who spend all their time telling people that the early Church
made up the idea that Jesus was God,
and deceived us.

Let me tell you an interesting thing about people.
If someone is a liar, a cheat, a swindler, or a crook,
they will assume
that the same things that motivate them
drive other people.
And you can always
spot a crook
by their accusations toward others.
The spirit of Anti-Christ
that denies God became a Man,
is first and foremost
the spirit of accusation.

As I have stated before, and will state here:
We believe in a revealed faith.

What we know about God,
has been told to us by God,
and so we have to believe that this revelation is true.

And that Truth is a person.
Not a set of precepts,
but rather a life
that has been witnessed to
by the gospel writers,
and the lives of the believers that followed them.

As Jesus said,
no one has ever seen God,
except the Son, and he testifies to what he has seen.

The Creed
defines who this Person,
Jesus Christ is.
And the only abstract section of the Creed,
the definition of who Jesus is
begins with Son.

There is one word that is used to describe this Sonship of Jesus.
Begotten.

Jesus is not created.
Nor is he birthed
in some strange myth
out of the head of the Father,
or out of the blood of conquered foes
like you read in Greek and Norse mythology.

Begotten is a mysterious word,
and in our modern world it is only found in John 3:16:
"God so loved the world that He gave His only begotten Son,
the whosoever believes in him should be saved."

Jesus is revealed out of the Father.

The Father is the Source,
and the Son is the revelation.
Jesus did not become the Son.
He did not have a moment of enlightenment
and discover he was the Son.
He didn't find plates in his garden
that said he was the son.
Nor did some guru come from the mountains
 and tell him he as the son.
Jesus was the Son from the beginning.
And because of this
he, and his message and ministry,
is completely and utterly unique in all of human history.

As John's Gospel begins:

> And the Word became flesh,
> and dwelt among us, full of grace and truth.
> We have beheld his glory,
> glory as of the only Son of the Father . . .
> And from his fullness we have received grace upon grace.
> For the Law was given through Moses;
> grace and truth came through Jesus Christ.
> No one has ever seen God;
> the only Son, who is in the bosom of the Father,
> he has made him known. (John 1:14-18)

So when we say Jesus is the only begotten Son of God
we are asserting several things.

Jesus shares at a deep level
the genetic makeup of the Father.
He bears the Image of the Father in the same way
a son would carry on the characteristics of a father in this world.
Jesus is the "spitting image" of his father.

Jesus bears an intimate relationship with the Father,
and communicates,

listens to, and responds
in the same way a healthy father and son would.

Jesus carries out and exercises the dominion of the Father.
Jesus is the heir-apparent
of the kingdom of the King of the Universe.
He functions in relationship to the Father
just as the
Prince of Wales relates
to the Monarch in the British Commonwealth.
Jesus has authority
due to his relationship to the Father.

And this is very important for us,
and for a Kingdom understanding
of the Sonship of Jesus.
When Jesus came
he made it clear
he came to establish
the Kingdom on earth
just as it is in heaven.

And for us believers,
Jesus being the Son of God
is extremely important.
Jesus tells us in John 3
that in order to come into the Kingdom
you have to be born into it.
It is an organic relationship,
just like his relationship with the Father.

And so,
as it says in Romans 8:1-17,
when we confess with our mouth Jesus is Lord
and believe in our hearts God raised him from the dead,
are baptized
and filled with the Holy Spirit,
the Spirit of Sonship comes into us.

Just like the Spirit of God
came into and rested on Jesus.
We are adopted,
and become children of God.
And we are brought
into the same relationship that Jesus has with the Father.
Jesus gives us access to his relationship.
We do nothing to receive this access.
He willingly gives us the access
and we cry
Abba Father.

And there are a lot of practical bits to this.

First,
the original sin was the breaking of the relationship with God.
When that relationship was violated,
the Holy Spirit left Adam.
He was still alive
but the LIFE of God left him.

When we are born by water and the Spirit,
we are brought back into relationship,
the life of God enters us,
and we begin to undo
the death that came in
when the relationship was broken.

This is why, when we are in the Kingdom,
we can pray for the sick
and they get healed.
It is not our power or our tricks that make it happen.
It isn't a magical incantation.
The Kingdom is not a religion,
but rather a new creation in the Holy Spirit.

No, we are in the Son, as the Son is in the Father,
and that life flowing through us brings the healing.

This is why we are told to
heal the sick,
raise the dead,
and preach the gospel.
We are not adherents to a religion.
We are members of a family.
And Jesus is the heir,
and he has invited us to be co-heirs.

This relationship surpasses
the relationship God had with Adam.
We are now invited into a
genetic,
intimate relationship
with the Father and the Son,
and we are invited to become one with them:
a living embodiment of wholeness,
life,
completeness,
and abundance.

And it is clear
in the seventeenth chapter
of the Gospel of John
that Jesus was praying
that we would come into this relationship,
so that we could share
that same relationship with each other.
We are only one with one another
when we are one with the Father.

God sent his Son
and interrupted human history
so that he might bring many sons to God.

We believe in One Lord Jesus Christ
the Only Begotten Son of God.

of one SUBSTANCE with the FATHER

Much of the church's teaching in this age
can be summed up in one word:
Inadequate.

We have come through a dark age where
the majority of Christians
have settled
for shallow
and "dumbed down" ideas
in exchange for entertainment and cultural relevance.

Any concept that is difficult to explain
and can't be put on a bumper sticker
gets ignored or simplified.

At the same time
we have pseudo-intellectuals
on all forms of media
spouting
some of the oldest heresies as new teaching
to promote the spirit of the age.

I hope that you have begun to recognize
that the men who wrote the Creeds
took all of this very seriously.
They were very careful
in how things were worded, and described.
And we forget a lot of history,
so I am going to recap a few important pieces here.

At the beginning of the fourth century
after the church came out from under the long persecution,
it was clear that there were many beliefs
circulating in the church.

Remember that in 325
the Bible as we know it
was not completely organized.

It would be over 100 years
before Jerome
translated the Greek into Latin
and created the first complete edition
of what we know as the Bible.
In 325 most congregations
had copies of parts of the New Testament.
Some churches had some parts,
and some churches had other parts.
The idea that one person would have
their own personal copy of the Bible
was an impossible idea.
The Gutenberg Bible was almost 1200 years into the future.

When you only have a portion of the New Testament,
you are going to miss things.
So there were churches that were like people today,
who only read one section of the Bible
and get off balance.

One important part of the Kingdom is balance.

Along with this,
many scrolls and books
were seized and destroyed during the persecutions,
so many people only knew key passages
and memorized prayers.

They knew the parts they heard during the Sunday liturgy,
and they knew the parts that were read in public,
but they were not able to go back
and get a sense of the whole picture.

And so,
there arose a number of ideas about Jesus
that tried to explain how he could be both God and man,
and how God could have suffered death and died.

Remember,
all heresy is man's attempt to reconcile great paradoxes.

So, Jesus is a very Jewish Messiah.
He is Emet.
Emet is a Hebrew word
that contains
the first,
last,
and middle letters
of the Hebrew alphabet.

It is the word for truth.
Jesus is the Beginning and the End,
and he is both fully man and fully God.
He is the living embodiment
of the Jewish belief
that truth is two seemingly opposite positions
that are some how
held together
in tension.
He is both man and God.

But to a Greek-Western mind,
who needs principles and precepts to argue,
and truth is a set of propositions that one agrees to,
this idea is ludicrous.

How can an
immutable,
omnipotent,
omnipresent,
transcendent,
sovereign being
feel pain and die?

And so there were many versions of a basic heresy:
Jesus the Human Being must be different than Christ the God.

And the loudest of those
at the time of the Creed was Arius,
who said that Jesus became God
and that he was of a similar substance to God,
but not quite God.

At the council
the orthodox position was defended by Athanasius.
Arius and Athanasius knew each other
and were both scholars at the schools in Alexandria.

This basic heresy,
that Jesus was not fully God,
is sometimes stated this way:
Jesus was in flesh until he died,
then he became a Spirit.
His resurrection was spiritual.
Because of this we can have enlightened
spiritual experiences.
His bodily resurrection doesn't matter.

Sometimes it is described this way:
God created Jesus
and called him the Son,
and Jesus experienced an epiphany
during life when he discovered he was God.
Because of this
he is one of the enlightened ones
like Buddha,
Confucious,
or Mohammed.

Many of these ideas come down to us
in liberal theology
and progressive or emergent Christianity.
(As well as the Jehovah's Witnesses
and the Mormons).

And so the Creed makes it very clear,
through a series of
seemingly repetitive statements
the core of Biblical Truth.

I mentioned earlier that the Creed
never references Greek philosophy,
but alludes to the Bible.
These statements are all biblical,
and either come from the mouth of Jesus or the gospels.
The council wanted to make it perfectly clear what the Bible
says about Jesus.

Jesus,
as I mentioned earlier,
is the Only begotten Son of God.
And as you study the creed,
you see that it is the theology written
in the Gospel of John,
and the letters of John
that have the most influence
over creed's wording.

So this section on the nature of Jesus begins with
Begotten of his Father
before all worlds.
Jesus was there
at the very beginning
with the Father.
That's John 2:2.

And the Creed makes it clear,
these were not two gods in a pantheon.
No,
the Father and the Son
were intrinsically related
from the beginning.

They were related before
the world,
the universe,
and every thing seen and unseen had a beginning.
How the Son is begotten we do not know,
but the Son was not the offspring of the Father
like the Mormons teach.
He was an expression of thé Father from all eternity.

God of God.
Jesus Christ did not become God.
His followers did not
rename him "Christ" after his death.
He was not an enlightened teacher.
He was not a self-proclaimed messiah.

No, he was the Son of Man
that Daniel saw in heaven in Daniel 7.
He is as much God as the One
Moses and the elders of Israel
saw on the mountain in Exodus 24.

Light of Light.
Jesus said in John 8:12
"I am the Light of the World."
In saying this,
he aligns himself with the Father
by calling himself I AM,
and alluding to the many references
to light in Scripture,
but most notably Psalm 36:9.
"You are the fountain of life,
in your light we see light."
John 1:4 says:
"In him was life,
and that life was the Light of Men.
The light shines in the darkness,
and the darkness does not overcome it."

Jesus is the Light.
He is the source of the Light.
He is not a reflection,
but the Light itself.
And his light is the Light of all humanity.
Any and all light that we have comes from him.
There is no darkness or mixture in this light.
This light dispels the darkness
and we are instructed
to walk in this light as He is in the light.
He is not
a shade,
a reflection,
or the mirror of the light.
He is the Source of the light, just like the Father.

And then to make it abundantly clear,
the Creed reinforces this point:
Very God from Very God.

We are building to a crescendo.
Jesus is not just God from God.
He is the true God
just like the Father.
He stands out among all Gods.
He carries the essential core reality
of what it is and means to be God.
This word "very" is about substance.
It is the true, the real, the full.
It is the unadulterated, unmixed, and purest form.
This phrase leads to the
most important sentence in the Creed.

Being of one substance with the Father.

Arius preached that Jesus was "homio-ousios"
like the substance of God, but not God.
A similar substance.

Athanasius,
who led the charge for orthodoxy,
taught that Jesus was "homo-ousios."
Of the **same substance** as the Father.

John tells us that Jesus is the Word,
and the Word was with God,
and the Word was God.
John must have learned this from Jesus himself.

In the 1970's
this line was translated "of one being with the Father."
This was a fudge to make the liberals happy.
One being and one substance really are not the same.
The new Roman Catholic translation says
"consubstantial."
It is accurate,
but not an easily accessible word to say or understand.
"Same substance" is what the Greek says,
and I think it makes it clear.

Jesus Christ is fully God.
God from God.
Light from Light,
True God from true God.
Begotten, not made,
of one substance with the Father.

These councils were raucous events,
and a fist fight broke out over this passage.
And after the council was over,
the decision was unpopular.
Arianism was the most popular form of Christianity
for about the next one hundred years.
When Athanasius died,
his epitaph read,
"Athanasius Contra Mundum"
Athanasius against the World.

He was the only orthodox bishop left when he died.

When my former denomination was beginning
to splinter apart,
and it was clear that false teaching was going to win,
and that the "conservatives" were
weak,
corrupt,
and pathetic,
and that my career was skidding to a dead end
before it was beginning,
it was the example of Athanasius
that kept me going.

There is an important thing my friend Kaye Gauder
taught me
many years ago in Akron.
"Truth and time go hand in hand."

Arianism died out.
No one knows why,
but I think I do.

It is a form of godliness with no power.
When you deny the deity of Christ,
you deny the power of the Gospel.
And it is interesting how any church
that removes the paradox,
the mystery,
and difficulty
from the God in the Flesh,
Jesus,
loses everything.

There is nothing deader
than a dead church or denomination.
It will truly suck the life out of you.
And this is the heart of the matter.

John,
who had the most influence
in the writing of this statement,
said that any person
who denied that Jesus was God in the flesh,
carried the spirit of Anti-Christ.
It is that simple.
And yes, it is black and white.
When you tolerate
and accept false teaching,
you are not being loving.
You are allowing death,
and evil,
to reign.

It does not take long to discover that this tree bears bad fruit.
Just look around.

I believe in One Lord,
Jesus Christ,
the Only begotten of Son of God.
Begotten of his Father,
before all worlds.
God of God.
Light of Light.
Very God of Very God.
Begotten not made.
Of One Substance with the Father.

77

ALL things WERE MADE through HIM

The section on the
nature and deity of Christ
ends with
with another reference
to the first chapter of the Gospel of John:
"All things were made through him,
and without him was not anything made,
that was made." (John 1:3)

Jesus Christ is the Maker of heaven and earth,
just as the Father is maker of heaven and earth.

300 years
after the Nicene Creed was written,
a group of Christians rose up
and began cutting the hands off
the artists
who painted icons.

Today we call this the "Iconoclast Controversy."
It was an ugly chapter in church history,
and it sadly was repeated again
during the Protestant Reformation.

Those who believe
that all forms of art and creation are idolatry,
fundamentally miss the heart of the matter:
The Christian is a little Christ,
and this Messiah
is God in the Flesh.
God with us.
And our Messiah is the creator of all that is, seen and unseen.
And as we transition to the section of the Creed about his life,
we shall see that the
Incarnation changes everything.

So let's look at this phrase:
Through Him all things were made.

Jesus Christ is the Eternal Artisan

Hebrews 13:8 tells us
"Jesus Christ is the same, yesterday, today, and forever."

In the charismatic streams of the church,
this verse is generally used
to win a theological argument
with people who believe
in the false teaching called cessationism.
Cessation
is the heretical idea
that miracles,
signs,
wonders,
and the supernatural
all ceased
when the Bible was completed.
And Hebrews 13:8 rightly tells us:
Jesus Christ still heals today.

But this verse is about something much bigger.
It's about the nature and character of Jesus Christ.
Before the Incarnation,
during his life on earth,
and now, in all eternity,
Jesus Christ is the same.
He never changed
when he became a man
from who he was before all creation.
And the Creed says:
Through Him all things were made.
Jesus Christ, Just like the Father, is Maker.

And this comes from John 1:3:
"all things were made through him,
and without him
nothing was made that was made."

Let's define a word:
Prior to the late 19th Century
the concept of the "artist"
was very different from today.

There were no "artists" as we understand them.
There were only artisans,
and they were members of a trade.
The primary job of the master artist
was to record historical events,
retell stories from history
and important cultural truths,
keep a record of collective cultural memory,
and record the images
of important members of the community,
like heroes, royalty, and saints.
Through painting,
storytelling,
song,
and theatre,
the artisan
kept the culture alive.

As it says in Ecclesiasticus 38:34
"They keep stable the fabric of the world,
and their prayer is the practice of their trade."

So if the true artist stops doing their true job,
the world goes into chaos and loses all stability.

So when you hear the word "artisan" in the Scripture,
this word means
painter, sculptor, weaver, potter, woodworker,
writer, scribe, and a thousand other applied crafts.
And this is the way I use the word.

So the Bible begins with God speaking the word,
and creating all things.

As I mentioned earlier,
the word for "call" is very important
in the first chapter of Genesis.
And from John 1,
we can assume that Jesus was the Word
that was spoken in that moment.
And when Genesis 1 refers
to "Us" and "We" in reference to God
we have to understand that Jesus
was there with the Father, and the Holy Spirit.

Jesus Christ is the source
of every creative miracle in the Bible.
He is, and was, first and foremost creator.
He was the Maker.

Jesus was one of the three visitors
who spoke the word to Abraham,
and Sarah conceived.

Jesus was the one
who led the Israelites out of bondage into freedom.

This is why when Jesus said in John 6:35
"I am the Bread that came down from heaven"
he was setting the record straight.
He was the source of the Manna.
He was the bread who sustained Israel,
so that not one of them were sick in the desert,
and none of their shoes wore out.
They were experiencing New Covenant reality
in the Old Covenant.

This is why Bezalel was called in Exodus chapters 31 and 35,
and is named the first Artisan in the Bible.

Bezalel was given an extraordinary list of gifts when he was
filled with the Holy Spirit:

Etching gem stones,
hammering gold
weaving cloth,
making dyes,
carving wood,
making incense,
and the ability to teach.
This is why Bezalel could construct something
exactly as Moses saw it on the mountain.
All these things pointed to Jesus the maker of all things.
There are thousands of books about Christ in the Tabernacle.

And when Jesus took flesh,
he learned a trade.
And he was the son of the carpenter.
He continued to be a maker in his earthly life.
The word in Greek that is translated "carpenter"
is not a builder of buildings and houses.

This is the word for "artisan with wood."
He was a fine craftsman and spent his time
carving utensils,
home implements,
fine furniture,
torah scrolls,
spice boxes,
and other wooden objects.

And of course,
Jesus created many things
during his earthly ministry:
water into wine,
bread for the multitudes,
opening blind eyes,
causing the lame to walk,
the deaf to hear,
and the dead to rise.
And he was a story teller and a culture maker.

And in his death and resurrection
Jesus established a New Covenant and a Kingdom.
And Paul said that he created a new creation.
He created a new day of worship,
the eighth day.

And then before he ascended
he told us he was going to continue making.
He was going to prepare a place for us.
He is making right now as you read this.
And Hebrews tells us that this place
is the place that Abraham saw,
all those thousands of years ago.
A city whose Master Architect
and creative designer is God.
The words in the Greek are artisan
and divine creative force.

And then we look at the end of the Bible,
in Revelation 21
we see a new creation.
A city made in heaven
of hammered gold,
and etched gemstones,
and filled with light and color
And kings from every culture will bring their glory into it.

It is the marriage of heaven and earth,
God and man.
The establishment of the Kingdom
under the rule of the King.

Jesus Christ is the same, yesterday, today and forever.

In several of my books
I talk about the shift we have made
into the next Christian era.

And I have said that the pastor
would no longer be the dominant leader of the church.

God is raising up artists and artisans
who will operate in the full five-fold ministry:
Apostles
who pioneer the Kingdom
in every realm of the arts and creativity.
Prophets
who reveal the true revelation of heaven
untainted by the world, the flesh, and the devil.
Evangelists
who declare the good news of the Kingdom
to those who have never heard it.
Teachers
who use their gifts to unpack Scripture
and lead people to maturity.
Pastors
who care for the poor,
the persecuted, the sick, and all who suffer.

And these five-fold artisans
are being raised up
to bring the Kingdom
and prepare the way for the return of the Lord.

As you can imagine, pastors didn't like what I said.
And the few publishers
and book reviewers to whom I sent my books
either refused to publish
or review it
or sent me full on abusive reviews.

But as I study Scripture,
and follow these threads,
the picture
in the original languages
is more and more clear.

God is the artist,
the designer,
the Author of Beauty,
the King of Creation,
and is preparing a thing for us
and we are his masterpiece.
We are little copies of the Icon of the Father.
God created us to be like him
and he wanted us to take a wild world
and make a Kingdom
where we could rule and reign with him
in beauty and honor
together.

Jesus Christ was both the image of the Father,
and the creator of masterpieces--
Little reflections of him
and his kingdom.

The highest calling
is to be a full,
whole,
integrated
artisan,
keeping the world together with your prayers.

It's not about quoting
Exodus 20:2 out of context
and telling artists to go get a real job.
We don't need anymore statues
being smashed by angry mobs.
The world,
the culture,
and the people all around you,
need you to do the thing inside of you.

Everything in this world
depends on it.

The only really effective [apology] for Christianity comes down to two arguments, the saints the church has produced, and the art that is grown in its womb. Better witness is borne to the Lord by the splendour of holiness and art which have arisen in the community of believers than by the clever excuses which apologetics has come up with to justify the dark sides, which, sadly, are so frequent in the church's human history.

If the church is to continue to transform and humanize the world, how can we dispense with beauty in our [worship], that beauty which is so closely linked with love and with the radiance of the resurrection? No. Christians must not be too easily satisfied. They must make their church into a place where beauty—and hence truth—is at home. Without this the world will become the first circle of hell.

From *The Ratzinger Report*, by then Cardinal Joseph Ratzinger, later Pope Benedict XIV.

You might be struggling with this.
And many of you may think
that God won't provide
or bless you
if you do what he told you to do.
Some of you are probably
not even sure if a calling to the arts is really from God,
because the message from the church
for centuries says the opposite.

You are created to bring heaven to earth
in a visible tangible way.
Jesus Christ is Lord over your life,
and Jesus Christ is the Master Artisan.

for us and our
SALVATION
HE CAME

Nearly 200 years ago
Darwin's theory appeared.
And it has now done something
Darwin would have never expected:
it has become a religion.

We live in a world that says
human beings evolved from nothing
for no apparent reason
in order to return to nothing.
The formal term for this is existentialism.

And so for many people
the question "Are you saved?"
Makes little or no sense.
Why would a nothing need saving?

This statement:
"for us and for our salvation."
Speaks directly to this question.
Saint Augustine said
that if you were the only human being in the world,
Jesus Christ would still come,
and still suffer and die
to save you.

You matter to God,
you have value.
And yes,
all of creation is going to be redeemed
as humanity is restored,
and takes it's rightful place over the earth,
but Jesus did not come for the animals
or the trees.
He came for us.
You are intrinsically different from the rest of creation.
You are not just a species.
You are not just something that evolved from a lower life form.

You were
created and made
in the Image of God.

Psalm 8 in the Hebrew
states you are a little lower than God,
and in Christ you are seated above all rule and authority.

You are valuable.
You were gifted with the ability to think, create, and be like God.
And you were designed to contain God.
No other creature in creation is like that.

But because of the breaking of relationship with God,
Adam and Eve became subject to the creation.
They came under the dominion of darkness,
and life would become toil and striving.

And here is one of the roots you need to understand.
Religion is the belief
that I have to do something to make God happy.
That is a return to the fall,
back to being expelled from Eden,
and back to trying to get back to where we once were.

You can never get back to Eden,
you can't make God happy.
As you remember,
the Trinity doesn't need you.
You can't make God sad or happy.
There are no tasks or disciplines
or works that will save you.

The Greek word "soter" is translated "salvation."
And in the Greek,
the various ways the word salvation
is used
give us this sense:

Salvation is not a one time event
when you go forward at the Billy Graham Crusade.
Salvation is an event
that is initiated
when we come to Christ,
and continues,
and increases,
throughout our lives,
and on into eternity.

Salvation is the continuous process of transformation,
sanctification,
healing,
maturity,
and endless becoming.

You become
more and more
who you are,
who you were created to be,
and who God intended you to be.
You get to be like the Skin Horse
in the *Velveteen Rabbit*,
who,
after having this hair rubbed off,
and his eyes fall out,
discovers he is real.

God wants you to be real,
not religious.
When you are religious,
and you measure your worth
by the stuff you do
for Jesus,
the church,
the invisible report card in your head,
or for the unhappy judge god you imagine.
Religion makes you more and more false.

Jesus Christ came down from heaven,
and short circuited that old lie,
that "I must do something to make Jesus happy."

Jesus is already happy.

When you do a bunch of things for Jesus,
you are saying,
in short,
"I don't want your salvation,
I will do it all myself."
This is how orphans think.

And Paul tells us in Galatians,
if you take on one part of the law:
trying to get there through your effort,
you take on the whole law
and come under a curse.

I'm sad for the Christians I meet who think
if they do all the right stuff
and work really hard,
then somebody will notice them,
and they will get recognized as a leader.
It never works,
and they get angry and resentful.

In the Kingdom
we can never work our way into the Kingdom.
This Kingdom doesn't work that way.
Jesus Christ came down from Heaven,
to take us there.
And what is very interesting to me,
is that many people
do not take his invitation to come into the Kingdom.
They think this invitation is too easy.
There must be a trick,
or a trap.

And for those of us who have learned the truth:
there is nothing in us that can move us forward,
that God wants a relationship,
and we must lean into him in order to move forward,
it is a constant adventure of
voluntary weakness,
submission,
and surrender.
This is how we move into the Kingdom.
We move forward in our salvation
just like Jesus did,
by choosing voluntary weakness,
going low,
leaving all our privilege,
and accepting the cross.

This week I told someone
that I do not say my prayers for Jesus.
Jesus doesn't need my prayers.
I need to say my prayers for me.
And that, I think, is the point.

Jesus displayed
on the holy Mountain that he was from heaven.
Peter, James and John saw Jesus return to his original state:
the Son of Man from Daniel 7,
with glorious raiment,
and a cloud of glory around him.
And the Father endorsed him.
This is my Beloved Son.

This is the Kingdom,
and this is the relationship.
And in that moment,
not only was Jesus exalted and honored,
but Peter, James, and John were exalted and honored.
They did nothing to get there,
other than follow Jesus.

There is one person in the
Transfiguration that I think we often overlook.
Moses.

There are a lot of reasons
why Moses and Elijah are with Jesus.
Neither of them left this earth the way most mortals do.
Their bodies did not face decay,
and both were taken by God.

But Moses never quite understood
this reality of salvation.
Paul tells us
that Moses put a veil over his face
to hide the fading glory,
and therefore put a veil
over the entire Jewish people,
who from then on saw the law
not as directions
to set them apart to make a holy nation,
but rather
a group of rules they must keep perfectly
to make God happy.

And because of this,
Moses got angry,
because when you fall into performance and effort,
you become angry,
and he whacked the rock instead of speaking to it.

Jesus was the rock he struck,
the source of living water.
And that kept him out of the promised land.
When you try to do things
you forget that God is holy,
and you do not strike holy things.
Performance creates an illusion that something in you
made it happen, and you begin to resent God.

When you play the performance game,
it always keeps you from the promised land.

It took a while,
but Moses did learn.
Because God is gracious,
and He is the most Relational Being in the Universe.
I can't imagine the feeling Moses had,
at the end of his life
to go all that way
and never set foot
in the place you led every one else to.

And so, here,
Jesus is on the Mountain,
and there are lots of things
people say
this appearance of Moses and Elijah mean.
But I know
for Moses,
it meant setting his foot in the Promised Land.

You are valuable to God,
and God really loves you and is for you.
God is really for everybody.
Religious people do not understand this.

And Jesus Christ,
as we will see over the next few weeks,
was willing to overcome and go through the very worst things
humanity ever devised
in order to save you.

It is very simple.
You are valuable,
You are precious,
and God will do anything
to help you get into the promised land.

HE took on FLESH

If you go to Nazareth in Israel,
in the basement
of the Basilica of the Annunciation,
is a stone building.

Archeologists have done many excavations,
and from what we can tell,
this is the oldest continuous
place of worship
in the Christian church.
It was first a house fellowship,
then a synagogue,
and then a basilica.
Graffiti scratched on the wall,
some of it nearly two thousand years old,
indicates that this was the home of Mary and Joseph,
and possibly the home of Mary before she was married.

In the middle of what once was a home,
is an altar built during the Counter-Reformation.
And the inscription on the altar reads
"Verbum Caro Hic Factum Est"
The Word became flesh, HERE.

And now we come to the problematic part for people.
The Bible is not a myth,
but a record of events in human history
with eternal consequences.

I work with artists in the hope
they will become disciples.
I quickly learned
that two things
were going to become a source of controversy:
the Holy Spirit,
and the Incarnation.

In order to be an Artist in the Kingdom
we have to let go
of some of the commonly held ideas
from the Protestant Reformation
and understand
that by the Holy Spirit
God took on flesh.

As Eugene Peterson says in the *Message*:
"God became a man and moved into the neighborhood."

And today in Nazareth,
you get a clear picture of the neighborhood
Jesus moved into:
Palestinian,
Jewish,
Arab,
and European people
all bumping up against one another.
It was this way during the time of Jesus,
because Nazareth was on a major trade route.

I am more and more convinced
that Joseph made things for trade,
simply because of the location.
The house in Nazareth is in the center of town
right on the major east-west trade road
from the fishing market on the Sea of Galilee
to the ports on the Mediterranean.

Jesus was a city boy,
not a country boy,
and probably fairly aware of the world around him.
All of these facts
become problems for spiritual Christians
who see Jesus walking by a stream,
surrounded by flowers,
and carrying a sheep.

The world of Jesus,
and the robe he wore,
was dirty, dusty, and probably a bit smelly.

Much of the religious world
believes in a form of Gnosticism:
Spirit is good,
and flesh is evil.
And so to say God took on flesh,
by the Holy Spirit,
turns this idea on its head.

And this quickly brings us back to religious ideas
about mortifying the flesh,
asceticism,
and again performance.
Gnosticism says
We have to work hard
to overcome the evil of the flesh,
and do stuff to be more spiritual,
to be good.
And if we do it well,
then we are "gooder" than other people.

Flesh,
from God's perspective
was never evil.
God didn't have to make flesh special
in order to prepare a place for Jesus.

In the 1925 film *Ben Hur*,
Mary is blond and blue eyed.
She goes into the stable in Bethlehem
with her serene glow and touches the wood.
"It is now sanctified" she says, and now she can have her baby.
They add little white doves for effect.
That's weird,
magical, and gnostic.

When God took on flesh
he was endorsing
the goodness of his creation in a profound way.
I once met the editor of *Christianity Today*,
Andy Crouch,
and he said that most Christians
read their Bibles from Genesis 3 to Revelation 19.
They begin with the Fall,
and end with the Lake of Fire.
The trouble is,
the Bible begins
with a Garden that is very good,
and ends
with a City that is beyond
our wildest hopes and dreams.
We live with God together, forever.

And this is the point of the Incarnation:
the Holy Spirit embodies himself in Jesus Christ.
In the flesh of Jesus,
the Holy Spirit made a dwelling place.
Because the Western Church
was too influenced by Augustine,
we have a very weak concept of the Holy Spirit,
and rely too much on Greek Philosophy.
St. Paul warned against this in Colossians 2:8.

And because of this,
we struggle with the Incarnation,
and we struggle with the Real Presence
of Christ in the Eucharist,
and we struggle with the power of God in the Christian life.
And for many Christians,
the faith is something you can talk about and think about,
but it has nothing to do
with how you live out your life in your flesh.
This is Greek thinking, gnostic thinking,
not Hebrew or New Testament.

The point is this:
the same Spirit
that was hovering over the waters in Creation
is the same Spirit that breathed into Adam
with the breath of life.

That same spirit filled Bezalel
and gave him the ability to build a replica
of the Kingdom on earth.

And that same creating life of God in the Holy Spirit
was wedded with the flesh of a human being
and she conceived.

And then that child,
a marriage of flesh and spirit,
born of the Holy Spirit and Flesh,
made a way in his own flesh
to allow us to be born of the Holy Spirit.

And his Presence,
Christ in us,
became a foretaste of the glory
we will one day experience in the new Jerusalem.
And this hope of glory:
Jesus Christ lives in you,
gives you the power to live in him,
and through him,
and with him.

As it says in Acts:
"In him we live, and move, and have our being."
And when we do this,
we can allow his life
to manifest in our flesh.

I do a lot of career counseling.
I find that some of our brothers and sisters

seem to always be struggling
with "missing the will of God."

For over thirty years I have heard this statement:
"I don't know if what I am doing is the will of God,
and so I don't know if I should stay here
or look for another job,
or quit my job, or what."

Some people,
especially artists,
think that what they do is inferior
to doing something spiritual
like becoming a missionary.
When Jesus became a man,
he didn't do anything spiritual.
He worked in a stinky, busy, middle eastern village.
He worked in a woodworking shop.
And from the reactions to the people who knew him,
probably had nothing about him
that made him unusual to the outside onlooker.

I recently had one of these career conversations with a friend
and I told him something he had never heard before:
God is pro-life in the fullest sense of what that means.
God loves your life.
God embraced your life.
And God endorses your life,
where ever you are.
God creates good things,
and his intention for you is good things.
Through the Holy Spirit
God can fill you in whatever it is you do:
artist,
automechanic,
mom,
computer engineer,
or creative professional.

God can come in the flesh
and fill what you do,
and Jesus who is blessed in all things,
can release blessing in and through you.

I am describing what Leanne Payne
called Incarnational Reality:
Jesus Christ by the Holy Spirit,
becomes flesh through us.
We can do the impossible
because he who did the impossible
can do things through us.

There is no striving.
In fact, effort and striving are expressions
of the Anti-Christ spirit.
We are back to religion,
back to trying to make God happy,
back to human effort and the curse.
Back to human solutions
that have two new problems
for every crummy, make-shift solution.

The Anti-Christ spirit,
the spirit of this age,
denies that Jesus Christ took on flesh.
This spirit says
"Jesus is a vapor giving you spiritual experiences
and you are left to sort everything else on your own."
It is all about your effort and your strength,
and no power from on high.
It is the spirit of slavery,
and accusation.

And this is the enemy
of every artist and creative person
in the Kingdom.

Every act of creation
begins with the Holy Spirit.
The Holy Spirit is the source.
And this of course relates to one of our core values:
Listen to the Lord and do what he tells you.

The one you are listening to is the Holy Spirit.
And trust me,
the Holy Spirit is always going to speak things
that are beyond your understanding.
The things the Holy Spirit speaks will give you life,
they will expand your faith,
and push you to step out into deep waters.
You will again and again be asked to take risks,
and you will again and again discover
you are weak without his strength.
And in living an incarnational life,
the Life of Jesus in You,
you will discover that God chooses
the weak things of this world to shame the strong,
the foolish things to confound the wise.

And again,
you will discover that our calling to be Christians:
little models of Jesus,
means every doctrine we mouth with our lips,
is a doctrine we expound and comment on with our lives.

By the Holy Spirit,
He took on flesh.
He emptied himself,
and clothed himself in complete humanity.
And because of this our complete humanity
can be filled with the Holy Spirit,
and we become something new.
A new Creation.
The Old is gone the new has come.

of the **VIRGIN MARY**

In my book
An Army Arising,
I talk about the 500 year shift that Christianity,
and by extension Western Civilization,
was about to experience.
Somewhere in these 15 years
a shift has begun.

If you have not gotten the message,
things are not going back to normal.

In the previous 500 years,
the church spoke to and tried to answer one question.
This question was
"What must I do to be saved?"

In the answers that were given,
it was the assumption of Protestant leaders,
that anything that did not obviously answer that question
needed to be removed
from the church,
its teaching,
and its practice.
For most Protestants,
this meant no images;
and for some,
no baptism and holy communion,
no confession,
no miracles,
no Holy Spirit (that is the doctrine of Cessationism),
and no Virgin Mary.

The movements that precede us
are marked by
smashing things,
removing things,
and looking for idols and demons
disguised in Christian garb.

And for artists
this has always posed a problem.

And of course,
the Counter Reformation,
during the Baroque era,
took all these things and made them badges of honor.
Even things that were not essential
suddenly came to be central:
Statues,
Paintings,
Music,
Saints,
and the Virgin Mary.

Now we know
both sides are answering questions
no one is asking anymore.

In 2006
when God told me to stop going to church
and sit in a coffee shop on Sunday,
I learned a lot
because I stopped telling people what to believe
and started listening.

I kept hearing different questions
than the ones I was given answers for.
The questions that kept coming up were
"What is my identity?"
"Do I have value?"
"Where do I belong?"

The answers I learned in seminary
do not answer these questions very well.
But orthodox,
biblical theology does answer them,
And the answers are really good.

And this is why we need to spend some time
looking at the Blessed Virgin Mary.

When I was a student
I became very interested
in the study of the liturgy,
and prepared to get my doctorate in it.
One of the reasons
liturgy became interesting to me
was it predates the Bible.
Worship is the place
where art and creativity interact
with the Holy Spirit.
Every move of the Holy Spirit in history gets recorded
in the worship of the Christian Church
through music,
prayers,
and traditions.

And you discover a lot of interesting things when you study the
liturgy.

Here is one of those surpises:
the first holiday added to the calendar
by Christians
was March 25,
the Annunciation.

This happened so early
there is no record of when it happened,
and we can assume that it happened during Mary's lifetime.
Like worship on Sunday,
it must have begun almost immediately
after the Ascension of Jesus.

And by an interesting coincidence,
the Annunciation and the crucifixion
happened on the same date.

And because we know the date,
we can date the day of the Resurrection,
March 28, 34 AD.

Holidays help create your identity,
and provide a place for you to belong.

The Kingdom is organic,
and the early Christians were not Western.
They were a tribal people.
They were a people of honor and relationship.

On one of my trips to Israel,
I met a man who was a Druze.
The Druze are descendants of Midian.
As we talked,
he told me that we were cousins.
He said that He was a descendant of Jethro,
and I was a descendant of Israel,
and Zsiporah,
Jethro's daughter,
was the wife of Moses,
so we were family.

We in the west do not think this way,
but the Biblical writers
and the writers of the Creeds did think this way.
And so it follows that Mary would receive honor,
and people would see Mary
as the "queen mother" of the tribe.
She was the mother of the chief,
and in a polygamous society,
the mother is more important than the wife.

And out of this understanding,
a tribal system of hospitality and honor
we understand what
Mary says in Luke 1:48,

"All generations will call me blessed."
in a completely different light.

Mary is a sign
and symbol of your value
as a human being,
She opened her body
to be the host of the greatest guest in history.
In doing this
she honored motherhood,
womanhood,
the human body,
and the human race in a completely unique way.

From the earliest days of the church,
there are references to Mary in statements of faith.
This is the third important Creed to refer to Mary,
and her virginity.
So we have to accept that to the earliest Christians
Mary was an essential part of the faith.

I remember a meeting
with an orthodox priest
at a ministry center in Boston.
He was explaining
the basics of the Greek Orthodox faith,
and some of the people in the room
were getting very upset
that Mary was understood
as an essential part of the faith.
With this,
the priest commented
that he preferred to not work with some Christians,
"because ignorance
and arrogance
are a deadly combination."

The Kingdom isn't about being right all the time.

For many ex- and anti-catholics,
Mary is a trigger point.
So we have some ground rules that we use
when we talk about Mary.

Every statement we make about Mary
must also say something about Jesus.
As the old saying goes,
"Mary is like the moon,
her only glory comes from the Son."

When I was studying icon painting
I learned there are many rules about icons of Mary.
Mary is never to be portrayed without Jesus.
Her life,
identity and place
in the church is defined
by the Son she bore and raised.

Every statement we say about Mary
must also be a statement that can be applied to us
because she is a member of the body.
She is a forerunner in the fullest sense of the word,
and Mary is not some kind of goddess.
She is a human being,
who was given an extraordinary honor.
And in being honored,
we also are raised up and exalted.

My own roots
are in a tradition that honors Mary,
and I think,
a tradition that also had a very balanced approach toward Mary.

Like many things in the spiritual life,
if we give them too much attention,
they will distract us and make us weird.

Just like fixations
on the demonic,
politics,
or any other wind of doctrine,
an obsession with Mary
will make you a bit weird,
and somewhat neurotic.

So many things in our lives are means of grace,
but all grace is a reflection of the true light
Jesus Christ.

To become obsessed with Mary
is like looking at the reflection
of a candle in the mirror,
rather than turning to the candle.
There is no denial that light
is coming forth from the reflection,
but it is not the light itself.
Jesus Christ is the true light,
and Mary was the vehicle
for that light to come into the world.

When I was learning about contemplation,
I discovered there were many themes
that are sources of
endless prayer and meditation.
Mary is one of those themes.
There are many themes
we could explore in talking about Mary,
but today I want to talk about just a few foundational ones.

The New Eve
In Genesis 3:8-15
we find the first Messianic promise in Scripture,
the seed of the woman will crush the head of the serpent.
The promise is given to Eve,
not Adam.

It will be the fruit of woman
that crushes the head of the serpent.
The theme of God providing a deliverer for his people
through a woman
is one of the most prominent ones in Scripture:
Sarah,
Sampson,
Hannah and Samuel,
the handmaid and David,
Elizabeth and John,
all point to
Mary and Jesus.

And when Mary sings the Magnificat,
it is heavily based on the song of Hannah in 1 Samuel 2.
And when John refers to Mary as Woman,
he is referring to her as the Woman
promised in Genesis 3.
Mary is the New Eve,
just as Jesus is the New Adam.
She is the mother of the new creation.

The first time Mary is mentioned
in the Church Fathers
outside the New Testament
is in 125 AD
 (The Gospel of John was completed around 90).
in the writings of St. Irenaeus.

This is the first reference to Mary as the New Eve.
Eve is approached by a fallen angel,
and is tempted.
Her response releases death into the earth.
Mary is approached by a holy angel,
and she too responds, and that response
releases eternal life.
Mary's response:
"let it be to me according to your word."

is the ultimate word of surrender to God,
and is a model for us to follow.

Spouse of the Holy Spirit.
In Luke 1 we encounter a word
that is technically called a
"Hapax Logemenon."

That is,
a word that appears once in history.
It is the word Gabriel uses to address Mary,
"kecharitomene."
This word,
often translated "full of grace,"
is unique,
and underscores that Mary
is really a unique being
in the history of the universe.
Mary is invited into the life of the Holy Trinity,
and because of this,
is full of grace.

Mary is the first person to embody the mystery of the Bride.
Let's not get lost in the mechanics of what happened.
Mary surrendered her body to the Holy Spirit,
and as Gabriel promised,
"The Holy Spirit would come upon her,
and the power of the most High would overshadow her,
and the thing which shall be born of her would be called Holy,
the Son of God." (Luke 1:34)

Mary is the first person in the New Covenant
to experience
the indwelling Holy Spirit.
And the life of the Holy Spirit
is so powerful,
she gives birth.

Like all things in the New Covenant,
we cannot understand them
without the Holy Spirit.
We cannot understand the Incarnation,
or the Virgin Birth,
without first understanding that
the Spirit of Life,
that breathed into Adam
breathed into Mary's womb,
and she conceived.

And that life in the Holy Spirit
continued through her pregnancy,
and through the raising of her Son.
Mary had to have been helped by the Holy Spirit,
in order to raise a whole functional person
who could be the Messiah.

And as we see throughout the gospels,
Mary is there at the important moments,
and is there at the day of Pentecost,
when the experience she has had
becomes the experience of all believers.
She is the Mother of the New Covenant.

Theotokos
As I mentioned earlier,
we cannot say anything about Mary
that doesn't also say something about Jesus.

Since we are discussing the Creeds,
we need to briefly mention
the Council of Ephesus in 431
where Mary was officially given a title.

If what we have said about Jesus so far:
God from God;
Light from Light,

true God from true God,
begotten not made
of one substance with the Father,
then,
He had to be all those things from his conception.
And this leads to a simple fact:
the church had to make a statement that Mary
was indeed the Mother of God,
or in the Greek:
Theotokos—the bearer of God.

And this leads to another thing that we need to accept.
If Jesus Christ truly is the Son of God,
then reality has been messed with a bit.
Christians believe that God has a mom.
Jesus calls a human being Mother,
and that relationship never ended.
And now we know from the study of DNA
that when a woman carries a son,
a bit of the son's DNA overrides the mother's
and he leaves a part of himself in her.
I will let that mess with you a bit.

And because the Kingdom is a Kingdom of honor,
Jesus honors his mother,
and we see this in his words from the cross,
Jesus saw to it that someone would look after his Mother.
This is a bit of a mind meld for some people.

And in being the God-bearer,
Mary does something
that we need to keep in mind,
especially as artists and creative people.
Mary undoes the gnostic idea
that flesh is evil and spirit is good.

She is the living embodiment of God
dwelling in flesh,

and her "yes,"
and her submission to God's will
is the ultimate act of creative expression
in all time, space, and eternity.
Mary is the mother of all creativity,
and God used her to bless the human body,
and bless physical reality.
The human body is good.
The created order is good.
Being fully a woman is good.

And for you to be called
to create and transform the world into
the Kingdom on earth,
you have to say "yes,"
and you have to submit,
and you have to surrender to God
in order to let God flow through you.
Mary is the model for the creative life.

Mother of all believers.
There are many biblical themes about Mary,
and most of them get revisited Revelation 11:19-12:17.

In this passage we see a woman,
who is first identified
as the Ark of the Covenant.
Then she is crowned with 12 stars,
the glory of Israel.
She wears a glorious robe
shining like the sun.
The moon is under her feet:
this could refer to the curse
referred to in Genesis 3.
And she gives birth to a male child,
one who will rule the nations with an iron scepter.
And it is this last description that helps us know
who this woman is.

It is Mary.

(Mind you, in Protestant seminary,
there were about seven interpretations of this image and
no matter what,
IT WAS NOT MARY!)

And this passage ends with this:
the serpent went off to make war on her children.

Who are these children?
They are us.
We are in relationship,
in this organic whole,
of the New Covenant.

The New Covenant is about relationship,
about being sons and daughters of God,
brothers and sisters of Jesus,
co-heirs of the Kingdom.
And this is a royal family.
Mary did not do anything
to achieve her place in this family
except for having favor with God,
and being willing to say "yes."
Because of this,
she has an exalted place in this family.
And we see a natural family order.
It's not about power or being right.
It's about family,
and honor.

One thing I have noted
in our brothers and sisters who do not honor Mary.
Their faith is brittle,
and they part company with others quite often.
The King of this Kingdom
is the Most Relational Being in the Universe.

The orthodox faith
is not rigid or brittle.
The true faith is flexible,
and can withstand stress.

It is based in life,
truth,
and holiness.
The Kingdom is a kingdom of honor,
and a body of believers filled with the Holy Spirit.
And in this we have relationship
with one another in
a mystical fellowship
much bigger,
and more profound than any other.

This relationship marks you.
You are part of a big family,
and this is where you belong.

The angel of the Lord declared unto Mary,
and she conceived by the Holy Spirit.
The Word became flesh
and dwelt among us.
We have seen his glory,
full of grace and truth.

HE was CRUCIFIED

In the old days,
every news article was boiled down to a few questions:
Who?
What?
Where?
When?
and
Why?

Everything in the Creed leads up to this sentence.
This sentence is the point,
and the crux
of the Creed.

If this man Jesus Christ
is all that we have said so far:
God from God
Light from Light,
true God from true God,
begotten not made
conceived by the Holy Spirit
born of the Virgin Mary
and fully man,
then,
this sentence is universe shattering.

Who:
Jesus Christ.
what:
Was crucified, died, and was buried.
Where:
In Jerusalem.
When:
During the governorship of Pontius Pilate.
Why:
For our sake.

Jesus Christ
the Incarnate Son of God,
died on a cross.

Crucifixion was the most horrible death
ever devised in human history.
At the time of the writing of the Nicene Creed,
it was still possible to travel every major road
in the Roman Empire
and see row upon row
of crucified criminals.
It was one of the greatest sources
of fear and shame across the empire.
The Romans used crucifixion
to make a spectacle of political rebels.

Crucifixion was the symbol of the Pax Romana:
If you disturb the power and peace of Rome,
then this is what will happen to you.
You will be stripped naked in public.
You will be flogged until your skin is ripped open.
You will be nailed to a cross,
and then you will hang there
while birds and pests eat at your exposed flesh,
people will mock you,
curse you,
or be repulsed by you in horror.
And you will eventually die
of a combination of exhaustion and suffocation
in your own blood.
It was the ultimate in cruel and unusual punishment.

And about 15 years after the Council of Nicea,
Constantine abolished the practice.

But the Creed not only mentions crucifixion,
but that Jesus
died.

God died.
The source of life,
gave up his life.
The one who made all things
submitted to torture and death at the hands of his creatures.

And God was buried.
God saw the inside of the tomb.
He who made the earth,
was received into the earth.
Really tortured.
Really dead.
Really buried.

And this happened not as a cosmic myth or metaphor,
but rather,
in real time
in a real place,
and by a real person.

The Romans were meticulous record keepers.
And up to the sack of Rome in the 5th century,
many Church Fathers mention
the records of the census in Bethlehem,
and the records of the career of Pontius Pilate.
And we know that Pilate was hated,
because there are doorsteps
in Israel
from the time of Jesus
with his name inscribed into them.
People wiped their feet on the name of Pontius Pilate.

This really happened.
And this will boggle your mind.
Jesus,
to fulfill the Scripture,
had to be in the tomb three full days.

That means that he had to have been crucified on a Wednesday
and laid in the tomb
at sundown.
And that means
that there had to have been a Passover
that began at Sundown on a Wednesday,
and that happened on
March 25, 34 AD.
The Day Jesus died on the cross.

These are real events,
and if all we have said about Jesus:
his nature,
his divinity,
and his coming to earth,
then this event,
the cross
is the most important event in human history.

The writers of the Creed make it clear:
He did it for our sake.
He did it for you,
and for me.
This is real,
and this is personal.
God died for you.

Jesus Christ took the promise of Passover to a nation,
that God would bring the victory
with an outstretched arm
and righteous right hand
and made it personal,
and possible,
for every human being to be brought into the Kingdom.

>   Why are your robes red
>   and your garments like one who treads the winepress?
>   I have trodden the winepress alone

and from the peoples
no one was with me.
For I have trodden them in my anger,
and trampled them in my fury.
Their blood is sprinkled upon my garments,
and I have stained all my robes.
For the day of vengeance is in my heart,
and the year of my redemption has come. . .
My own arm brought salvation for me,
and my own fury sustained me.
(Isaiah 63:2-5)

Set me as a seal upon your heart,
As a seal upon your arm,
For Love is strong as death,
Jealousy cruel as the grave.
Its flames are flames of fire,
and it passions as the unquenchable flame.
Many waters cannot quench love,
neither can the floods drown it.
(Song of Songs, 7:6-7)

Surely he has borne our griefs
and carried our sorrows.
Yet we esteemed him stricken,
smitten by God and afflicted.
But he was wounded for our transgressions,
and He was bruised for our iniquities.
The chastisement
that brought us peace was upon him,
by His stripes we are healed.
All we like sheep have gone astray,
We have turned,
everyone until his own way;
and the Lord has laid on him the iniquity of us all.

Jesus Christ took upon himself our sin
and the fullness of the broken relationship

between God and Creation
in order to establish a Kingdom,
and to bring many children to God.

Have this mind among yourselves,
which was in Christ Jesus,
who, though he was in the form of God,
did not count equality with God a thing to be grasped,
but emptied himself,
taking the form of a servant,
being born in the likeness of men.
And being found in human form he humbled himself
and became obedient unto death,
even death on a cross.
Therefore God has highly exalted him
and bestowed on him the name which
is above every name,
that at the name of Jesus every knee should bow,
in heaven and on earth and under the earth,
and every tongue confess that Jesus Christ is Lord,
to the glory of God the Father.
(Philippians 2:5-11)

And in this is the principle spiritual law of the Kingdom,
and by extension the whole Universe.
You must die in order to live.
A seed must fall to the ground
and die before it can bear fruit.

As Jesus himself tells us:
"Whoever desires to come after me,
let him deny himself,
take up his cross and follow me.
For whoever desires to save his life will lose it,
but whoever loses his life
for My sake and the kingdom,
will save it."
(Mark 8:34-35)

St. Paul said
he did not come with the world's system or values,
but rather with the power of God.
Paul didn't use his credentials,
or the established system,
or rhetoric,
or marketing.
Instead, he preached the cross
in the power of the Holy Spirit.
Isaiah tells us there was nothing
about Jesus that made him attractive.

Often you hear people preaching
that the cross is some kind of difficulty
like a difficult boss
or a boring spouse,
and we have to bear this as some kind of purgation on earth.
This is not the Kingdom.
This is the world's thinking.

The Kingdom is not about bearing a life
of misery,
having a martyr complex,
and calling it a cross.
The Kingdom is transactional.
I lay down my life
and surrender it to God,
and in my moment of emptiness,
God gives me back my life
and fills it with resurrection power.

I lay down my will,
in exchange for the will of the Father,
and I receive
the fullness of the Kingdom.
I trade my desires
for the desire of God.

Jesus emptied himself
and embraced the death of a criminal
and in dying
gave us life.

I invite you,
to meditate on the cross and passion of Jesus
to embrace the crucified life—
a life of surrender to Jesus.

When Christ calls us,
he calls us to come and die.
Jesus wants everything,
but in giving him it all,
we get everything and more in return.

Come be a disciple of Jesus,
invite him to be the Lord of your life,
and let him take your life
and turn it into something beautiful for God.

HE ROSE

This phrase is the foundation
of the New Covenant and the Kingdom.
The New Covenant
would have been a nice religious idea
if Jesus had not risen,
this would have been another movement
by another upstart rabbi,
and Jesus would have been a footnote in Jewish history,
and probably have been forgotten.
This rabbi was martyred like so many others.
But then Jesus rose from the dead
like he said he would.

When Jesus rose from the dead
he confirmed and established
that the New Covenant and the Kingdom are real.
He confirmed it in his own body.

With this sentence,
and the next one "He ascended,"
the verbs change in the Creed.
We move from looking back into the past
to looking to the present-future.
Kingdom resurrection time is present-future.
It is always "Kairos" time in the Kingdom.

To the ancient Greeks there were two kinds of time.
"Chronos" was depicted as an old man
who labors monotonously
under the weight of fleeting time.
Chronos has come down to us as "Father Time,"
the old man at the end of the year.
"Kairos" was different:
it was that pregnant moment of opportunity,
and great things.
In the Kingdom it is always kairos.
Every moment is pregnant
because God messed with the time space reality.

The phrase "the third day" appears 84 times in the Bible.
And to just give you a sense of it's importance:

On the third day God separated the earth from the water
and caused all green plants to grow.

On the third day Abraham took Isaac up to Mount Moriah to
sacrifice.

On the third day the people of Israel walked through the Red
Sea into freedom.

On the third day the elders of Israel climbed the mountain with
Moses and ate and drank with God.

On the third day Jonah was released from the belly of the whale.

On the third day Jesus went to a wedding at Cana in Galilee and
turned the water into wine.

On the third day Paul was baptized and received back his sight.

And of course, on the third day Jesus Christ rose from the dead.

And in Scripture,
"day" is much broader than a 24 hour period.
It is we "post-enlightenment" people
who rigidly define everything in life.

For most of human history a "day" could be understood
as an era,
or an epoch of time.

And so the Bible understands days
this way many times and in many places.
The first day was the time from Adam to Moses.
The second day was the time from Moses to Jesus.
and Jesus arose on the third day, the "last day."

This day is the Day of the Lord,
the Day that begins with Jesus rising again
and will end when Jesus returns.
This is the Lord's Day.

And of course,
in terms of the days of the week,
Jesus rose not just on the third day,
but he rose on the "eighth day,"
the first day of the new cosmic reality.
Jesus is the last Adam who has undone the fall.
And eight, to the Biblical writer,
is a sign of a rebirth,
or a new beginning.
It is a sign of eternal life.
And so when you go into an old church,
you find the Baptistry
has eight sides.

And this is where we are going--
When Jesus walked out of the tomb,
he was not a resuscitated corpse.
He was something completely new,
something that never existed before.

Let me say this again:
When Jesus Christ came out of the tomb
he was something that never existed before.
A human being unable to die.
Jesus Christ undid the second law of thermodynamics:
All matter moves from a state of order to disorder.
Jesus arose from a place disorder and created order: Shalom.

In Hebrews 4 it is clear,
there is a place of Shalom rest that exists
at all times for the believer,
and that place is Jesus Christ himself.
He is our shalom.

And Shalom is the first benefit of the resurrection.
And when he rose from the dead he became our Shabbat.
Our rest went from a day
to a person,
and when we dwell in him,
and let his life flow out of us,
his rest can manifest
not only to us,
but through us.

In the beginning
God took the dust of the earth,
carbon and water mostly,
mud.
And he breathed into that the breath of life.
Interestingly,
the word "adam" means "mud" in Hebrew,
and scientific research has learned
that human beings are mostly carbon and water.

And so God took mud and the Holy Spirit:
the breath of God,
the breath of Life
entered into the mud
and Adam became a living being.

And we know,
that didn't work out so well,
because the creature was created
from something that was not living.
And when the life source was cut off,
the breath of life,
Adam died.

Death always results when our relationship with God is severed.
But even in the moment death entered the world,
God promised that the curse would be reversed.

Fast forward unknown numbers of years,
and we are in a cold stone tomb.

There is a body,
bruised,
broken,
bleeding,
and battered.
And once again,
the Holy Spirit
breathed into this body,
not a lump of mud,
but a body that had once been filled with the Holy Spirit.
A body that had performed miracles,
been transfigured and walked on water.
A body that had been wounded for our iniquities,
and pierced for our transgressions.
And this time the Breath of Life
entered a body in perfect relationship with God.
The relationship was never severed.
And this body could not fall
or break that relationship,
but instead
was risen in perfect relationship.
And this perfect relationship,
in broken flesh
was able to unlock a new kind of being.
And something new was created.

As Paul says in II Corinthians 5:17
If anyone is in Christ
they are a NEW CREATION
the old is gone and the new is come.

The New Testament does odd things with verb tenses.
Jesus wasn't raised, he is raised.
Christ has died
Christ is risen.

From the moment Jesus walked out of the tomb,
the Kingdom was moving forward,
not looking backward.
Because of the resurrection
the Kingdom is present-future.

The Old Covenant was.
We looked back to Moses and David.
The New Covenant and the Kingdom is and will be.
The Old Covenant was death,
and Old Covenant prophetic ministry
was a ministry of death.
The New Covenant is life in Christ Jesus
and the prophetic is a present future ministry of life.
The Old Covenant said a dead person would make you unclean,
and in the New Covenant a resurrected person
can make you clean.

He who entered the fullness of suffering,
punishment, and bondage,
rose from the dead,
and is able to not only set millions free,
but also allow that power to flow through the freed
to set others free.
by the same Spirit that raised him from the dead.

And in the rising several things happened:
His body became a new form of life.
He was now a higher physical life form.
He was able to walk through doors,
and there is evidence from the Shroud of Turin
that the body
may have passed
through the grave clothes as he was resurrected.
Something happened at the quantum level.

Paul says in I Corinthians 15
that Jesus died a human being in the flesh,

but rose a spiritual being.
And from what we can tell
in the New Testament
after the resurrection
he is not a ghost,
but actually a being stronger than physical.
He is not a shade of this life,
but this life is a shadow of him.

His body became fully a temple of the Holy Spirit,
a container for God in a way not possible before.
He was able to convey the Holy Spirit to people.
Jesus breathed on them
and they were filled with the Holy Spirit.
And in being filled, he made them temples as well.

He was able to pass from this reality to the next one,
to go to the Father,
and to ascend into heaven.

He is no longer bound by time and space.
He is able to appear to people
beginning with Paul on the road to Damascus
and continuing throughout history:
Jesus has appeared to
and ministered to all his apostles throughout history.
And from the book of Acts we know that
Philip was also suddenly no longer bound
by time and space in the Holy Spirit.

And as I said before,
When Jesus Christ came out of the tomb
he was something that never existed before.
A human being who was unable to die.

Jesus Christ undid the second law of thermodynamics:
All matter moves from a state of order to disorder.
Jesus arose from a place disorder and created order.

And not only did he move from disorder to order,
he created a higher order.

This means that he began the process
of reversing the old order of sin and death.
It means that we can speak to sick people
and they will be healed.
And it means that God can release to you
all the blessings promised as his intent for Israel.

Jesus Christ's first word
after his resurrection to his apostles was "Shalom."

Shalom is not the Western idea of peace:
peace is not the absence of conflict
or the avoidance of trouble--
that's a vacuum.
And nature abhors a vacuum.

Whenever there is that kind of peace,
there is a vacuum
that gets filled with worse trouble.

Shalom is fullness of order,
not the absence of trouble.

God fills things
with his own resurrection life
and takes territory.
Shalom is order.
Shalom is no brokenness.
Shalom is rest.
Shalom is wholeness.
Shalom is material prosperity
to the point that you have no concerns
and can be a blessing to others.
Shalom is righteous relationship.
Shalom is contentment.

Jesus Christ rose from the dead,
and as he demonstrated in his ministry,
God gave him the ability to forgive sins.
And in the resurrection,
Jesus tells his disciples,
I give you this ability as well, in the Holy Spirit.
And with a word,
sins can be erased.

This is the promise of the resurrection:
righteousness,
peace,
and joy in the Holy Spirit.

And this promise,
because we are a present-future people,
is that one day
we too will rise
and we too will be incorruptible
in an unbroken relationship with God
and with each other.

When Jesus Christ rose from the dead,
in the rising was a commission:
This reality is so important
that it must be shared and declared.
"As the Father has sent me,
so send I you." (John 20:21)

As Matthew puts it:
"All authority has been given to me."

Jesus is the
King of the Kingdom,
any and all authority
we have
comes from him.

Therefore,
go and make disciples--
not "Jesus followers,"
not converts,
not people who repeat a prayer
with every head bowed and every eye closed,
not bums on seats
or big churches and ministries.

No,
people who have said,
I will take up my cross Jesus and follow you.
I will die with you so I can be full of resurrection life.
I will surrender to you,
because you were dead and now you are risen
and that changes everything.

Baptize them
in the Name of the Father and the Son and the Holy Spirit.
Birth new beings into this new creation
by water and the Holy Spirit.
And teach them to observe
all that I commanded you:
love one another.

In 2006 our fellowship, Belonging House,
began the journey of
going into an unreached people group:
the realm of the arts and creativity.
Satan hates this.
The last thing he wants are people
who are disciples in his turf
changing the way people think.
He has almost completely succeeded
in making this world hell on earth.

Satan hates what we are doing
and the past few months have reminded me

that anything
that you make more important
than the Kingdom:
finances,
politics,
morality,
or religious games,
will become an idol,
and you can become full of demonic power,
and you will do evil thinking you are doing the work of God.

Jesus warned us about this.
The people who crucified him
were the "good people."
Saul was a "good guy" who helped stone Stephen,
the first Christian martyr.

Jesus the risen king really doesn't care about
your goodness or your Christian credentials.
He cares that you are submitted to his Lordship.
Recently,
we have seen more fruit
in the original mission
than anytime before,
and oddly,
good Christians
have caused me more trouble than anytime before.

Anytime you are going
in the right direction as an artist,
you will face resistance.
We are going in the right direction,
and so Lord,
we ask you today to breathe on us again
like you did in the upper room.
We need the Breath of God
to fill us anew and afresh
to continue to be sent.

We ask you to breathe on all
who are reading this book
and we ask you to blow on them
like the seeds of a dandelion
that they would be carried
to the four winds and produce
a meadow of disciples.

We ask you to breathe on us
the resurrection life,
and fill us to share this good news
with those we know in darkness
who are confused and afraid,
and who have lost hope.

On the third day he rose again from the dead.

Alleluia,
Christ is Risen,
the Lord is risen indeed,
Alleluia.

in accordance
with the
SCRIPTURE

Because of the Resurrection,
we believe in the Bible.

One of the most interesting stories in the Bible
takes place in the afternoon
after the resurrection.
There are two disciples
on the road to Emmaus.
They had gone to Jerusalem
for the Passover,
"a feast of ascents"
a feast that requires you to make a pilgrimage
to Jerusalem and sacrifice at the Temple.

And so on the day of Preparation for the Passover,
the crowds of pilgrims are exposed
to a truly horrible
scene.

Jesus,
the prophet from Galilee,
the wonder worker
that the vast majority of the people had begun to follow
was being led through the city
carrying his own cross
(an especially brutal addition to the punishment)
to send a message to everyone:
don't make yourself into the King of the Jews
and don't follow him or else this will happen to you.

And so
everyone in Jerusalem
celebrated the Passover
and the Sabbath that followed
together
having to experience and be reminded of this truth:
it is very dangerous to be a Jew.

And these two disciples were depressed.
They were discussing what they had seen
and heard in Jerusalem.
As often happens on a journey,
you meet someone along the way
and begin having a conversation as you travel.
And this person seemed to not know
about what happened over Passover.

And he began to tell them,
beginning with Genesis
all the places in the Bible
that pointed to the death
and resurrection of the Messiah.

And when they reached the house
they invited him in,
because in this world hospitality is an ethic of life.
And since it appeared that he was a rabbi,
they let him bless the matzah,
and when he did
they knew him in the breaking of the bread.

And then he was gone.

There is an unbroken liturgical tradition
from this point on
of the intrinsic link
between the Bible and Holy Communion.
I believe this story
is the embryo of the Easter Vigil
where each year we hear
many of the stories Jesus probably told
the two disciples on the road to Emmaus.

The Creed adds a statement
that is an addition to all the previous Creeds:
"He rose from the dead in accordance with the Scriptures."

We Believe in the Bible
because of the Resurrection.

St. Paul writes in the second letter to Timothy:

> But as for you, continue in what you have learned and
> have firmly believed, knowing from whom you learned it
> and how from childhood you have been acquainted with
> the sacred writings which are able to instruct you for
> salvation through faith in Christ Jesus. All Scripture is
> inspired by God and profitable for teaching, for reproof,
> for correction, and for training in righteousness, that the
> man of God may be complete, equipped for every good
> work. (II Timothy 3:14-17)

Paul probably would have been surprised
that his letter is now considered part of Holy Scripture.
By 325 the church had added this,
and many more of Paul's letters
to the list of sacred writings.
They thought it was inspired.

Scripture is inspired.
In other words,
the Holy Spirit communicated to and through the writers.

Some places,
like in the prophets
this is obvious.
They say something
and end with "Thus saith the Lord."

Some of them,
like the stories in Genesis,
were oral tradition
conveyed around camp fires at night
for centuries
before scribes took the time to write them down.

And other places,
like the long genealogies in I Chronicles,
don't seem inspired at all,
and so we skip them.
And then a guy writes a book called the *Prayer of Jabez*
and sells millions of copies.

It was inspired.

The Holy Spirit was in the process
from the first person who received the word
to the sharing of the word in the community
to the writing down of the word by scribes in Babylon
and the editing and transmission from copy to copy
to the translators
to the many versions
to the publishers
to the bookseller.

Everywhere this book goes it is living and powerful,
so that David Suchet sitting in a hotel,
bored after a long day on a film set,
pulls the Gideon Bible out of the nightstand
and reads
Paul's letter to the Romans
and becomes a believer.

The Bible he read was a crummy translation
with a crummy typeface and a cheap binding.
And it changed his life forever.

The Bible is like Jesus--
it is both human
and it is full of God.
This is why it so effectively points to him.
But Jesus warned us,
the Bible is not an end in itself–the Bible always points to him.
The Bible is incarnational.

It is an Icon.
And it is a work of art.
It contains
poetry,
a play,
at least one clear intended work of fiction,
stories,
narrative history,
and
a lot of sex and violence.

When you get a full understanding
of how living and active this word is,
this written record of God speaking to us,
and how vibrant and dynamic it is,
you will not be threatened
when unbelievers say stupid things about it.
They think this is a human book
composed by deceptive people
to make converts.
That should be your first clue into their motives.

And because they think the people who wrote this book
have the same motives they do,
they see deception everywhere.
And this is the beginning of wisdom.
Generally a person who accuses you of ridiculous things
is doing those things themselves.

You will never see the treasure in this book
until you have faith in the Author.
This is the veil Paul talked about,
and why there are libraries of Jewish
and Christian commentaries
that have so little life in them.
If you do not read this book in the power of the Holy Spirit,
you will never get the fullness of it.

So why does the Bible have authority?
Jesus pointed out on the road to Emmaus
that this continuous story is full of forward looking promises,
and there is an astounding
track record
of the promises
coming true.

Abraham's sons have both produced great nations.
God brought those nations to the land God showed him.
Israel went into slavery.
Israel was rescued from slavery.
Israel was again sent into exile
and told they would be brought back to their land.
They went back.
And then they were exiled again and told they would one day
come back again.
And now they are there.
That series of events alone
is beyond human statistics.
David described
the crucifixion in Psalm 22
1000 years before it happened,
and Isaiah spoke
in detail of the Messiah 800 years before the birth of Jesus.

The Bible has authority
because whenever someone interacts with it,
God speaks.

And when God speaks it changes you and bears fruit.
I knew of a man
who was a world renowned scholar of Leviticus.
I think he was a Presbyterian
who didn't believe in the supernatural.
And yet, he was hearing God speak to him all the time
through Leviticus
in ways that were beyond his understanding.

This book is mysterious,
and it contains eternity.

God gives this book authority.
And we submit to this book out of our submission to God.

Often religious people try to keep this book
from having authority
or diminish its importance.

Fools and children
read it
and have encounters with God.
Religious professionals
correct them,
tell them "that isn't so,"
and command them to submit
to their earthborn authority.
The most blasphemous stuff
I have ever read came from academic biblical experts.

In the 1940's the Bishop of Colorado
was on a train going over the Rockies
and he was put into a cabin with a Baptist minister.
When the Bishop took out his prayer book
to do his readings for morning prayer,
the minister noted,
and said, "My church is based on the Bible."
The bishop, without looking up from his reading said,
"My church wrote it."

This is the paradox of the Incarnation:
God used people to create this book,
and the church existed before the New Testament.
There is a tension in this.
It is very dangerous
to believe that any religious institution or authority
gives this book authority.

Although the book came from the community,
the community does not have authority over it.

The Church never stands above Scripture.
When someone takes this position,
they eventually hold the Bible in contempt.

An equally dangerous position is to give the
Bible authority based on
authorship,
inerrancy,
and infallibility.
It is dangerous to say things
about the Bible
that the Bible doesn't say about itself.

This book does not claim
unquestioned authority on every page.
The Bible is very sure of its identity,
and doesn't need you or anyone else
to defend it.
This position will lead to idolatry.

Somewhere in the Middle Ages the idea developed
that the Bible gets its authority from authorship.
This belief was an easy target to dismantle,
and liberals first whacked Moses in the 19th Century,
then they came up with three Isaiahs,
and now the Jesus Seminar has determined
through colored marbles,
that Jesus didn't say anything except
Love is love.
Remember what I said about motives.

Scholars have also attacked the idea of inerrancy.
It is very hard to defend the idea that the Bible has no errors.
This is a Jewish book,
and it is full of contradictions.

Jesus says blessed are the peace makers
and then says go buy a sword.

When I was doing an intense study on Bezalel,
I discovered that Exodus 37:1 and Deuteronomy 10:5
clearly contradict.
I discovered a textual problem
in the 36th chapter of Exodus.
From what I could tell,
there was a chunk of the text missing,
and then a later scribe came in and finished the story,
erasing Bezalel and replacing him with Moses.
He mentions a coin in use
during the Second Temple period,
not the time of the Exodus.
That's a problem.
And no one wrote about it in the commentaries.
And since it was about art,
they had no desire to work through the problems.

You are going to find problems in a 4000 year old book.
This book is God's inspired word
with human fingerprints all over it.

In the process of wrestling with these issues,
I learned a lot about God,
and how big God is.
The Lord has let all these people,
often with conflicting opinions and agendas
work on his Word.
And when you dig,
you see he is not threatened by any human motive.
God is bigger.
Rather than shake my faith,
my faith in this book increased.

Infallibility
means that there is no error in any teaching.

And this gets a bit murky when you do find minor issues.
So they add caveats,
like in the original
(something we cannot possibly have),
or in the most correct manuscripts.
Again,
we must not say things about the Bible
the Bible does not claim for it self.

One of the big helps for me
was discovering how
the orthodox Jewish community handled
the obvious problems in the Torah.
They believe this book was created out of the community,
and it is the responsibility of the community to carry this story.
We are the people of the Book.
This is our book,
it is not a book over us,
but a book that was given through us.
The greatest way to express the truth of this book
is not by winning arguments
but by how this book is lived out in our lives.

What the Bible claims is this:
That it is inspired.
It points to Jesus.
It is living and active,
sharper than any two edged sword.
It is powerful,
will produce fruit and not return void.
And it will stand forever.

And all these claims have proven true.

So what should our relationship to the Bible be?
I believe we should be reading the Bible daily.
I use the method worked out over centuries,
the daily office Lectionary.

When you are in the Scripture,
you learn how God speaks,
and this process creates
a "landing strip"
or a runway
in our hearts
to receive his word
in our lives on a regular basis.

When we come to a place
that is hard to understand or is confusing,
I suggest you do several things.

First pray,
"God, what does THAT mean?"

Second, go to the original language.
There are lots of good Bible resources online
that can help you discover the original,
even without knowledge of Greek and Hebrew.

Third, go to a reliable source
who might have the answer, or insight.
I also read what reliable sources have said throughout history.
One of the best study Bibles
to do this is the one created by Scott Hahn,
the *Ignatius Study Bible New Testament*.

And sometimes,
you just have to wrestle with the Bible and live with it.

Zechariah 1:18-2:2 is one of those passages
that I wrestled with for over a year.
It became my book *An Army Arising*.

When you engage in this process,
God starts to change you.
And I think that's the point.

Because the Bible is inspired by the Holy Spirit,
we believe it has authority.

This book tells us how
God has talked in the past.
How God has revealed himself in Jesus Christ,
and how people have interacted with God
without getting themselves killed.

John Wesley said
that the Church must be constantly reforming.
He saw and understood that human beings
quickly go from order to disorder,
and when you build traditions
around a previous reformation,
they quickly become corrupt movements
that also need reforming.

The only way to reform is to
keep coming back to this book,
realigning yourself with its contents,
and letting God cleanse you with his word.
The Bible is the most powerful reforming agent we have.
And when we let it penetrate the closed gates of our hearts,
God inspires us
and transforms us.
And the promise of the resurrection continues.

When I was a student,
the book *Prophet with Honor,*
the official biography of Billy Graham,
was released.
Early in his career, Billy Graham
and another young man,
Chuck Templeton,
were the leading speakers
for Youth for Christ.

A group from the National Council of Churches
made them each an offer.
They were promised more access to mainline churches,
if they adopted the liberal view of the Bible.
Chuck Templeton bit the apple,
attended Princeton Theological Seminary,
and was quickly offered opportunities
to speak to youth gatherings
in several denominational churches.
Eventually he became an agnostic.

On the other hand,
Billy Graham went for a walk in the woods
and got down on his knees.
He took his Bible in his hands and promised God
he would "take the Bible by faith
and preach it without reservation."

He graciously turned
the National Council of Churches
down.
And as you know,
Billy Graham preached to more people
than any other person in Christian history.

After I read that,
I did the same thing,
I got down on my knees
in my dormitory at Asbury
and prayed a similar prayer.
That basic surrender to God's authority in the Bible
has gotten me through face-offs with bishops,
arguments with snotty art professors,
and a denominational split.
I know that this book is true.
And if you want to make a difference in this world,
you have to settle this issue.

Because Jesus Christ
rose from the dead,
he could look back and say,
"see it was all true."
It happened just like God said it would.

And because of that we can say—
I believe
and live
in accordance with the Scriptures.

Because of the Resurrection
I believe in the Bible.

HE ASCENDED into heaven

The most quoted verse from the Old Testament
in the New Testament
is Psalm 110:1.
"The LORD said to my Lord,
Sit at my right hand,
until I make your enemies your footstool."

To the first Christians
the most important event in life of Jesus
was the Ascension.

Many people think that Christianity
is an historic religion
that believes in events in the past.

It's not.

Christianity is a living faith
that practices a spiritual reality.
This reality is rooted in the fact that
human beings who
were once separated from God
can now have
a current relationship with God.
The past events made this present reality possible.

After Jesus Christ died and rose again,
he ascended into heaven,
and he is there right now.
And that makes everything in the Christian life possible.

Many people think that eternity is a long time.
Actually,
eternity is outside of time.
It is another reality,
beyond the linear realm we live in.
So, when Jesus left time,
he went into eternity.

And because he is outside time,
he can be in all times and at all places
at once.

As we have said earlier,
Jesus Christ is God
and fully man.
And Jesus referred to himself
by one title more than any other:
Son of Man.
Jesus is the Son of Man.
And this is a reference to Daniel 7:13.

> I saw in the night visions,
> and behold, with the clouds of heaven
> there came one like a son of man,
> and he came to the Ancient of Days
> and was presented before him.
> And to him was given dominion
> and glory and kingdom,
> that all peoples, nations, and languages
> should serve him;
> his dominion is an everlasting dominion,
> which shall not pass away,
> and his kingdom one
> that shall not be destroyed.

This is the other side of Acts 1:9-11.

> And when he had said this, as they were looking on, he
> was lifted up, and a cloud took him out of their sight.
> And while they were gazing into heaven as he went,
> behold, two men stood by them in white robes, and said,
> "Men of Galilee, why do you stand looking into heaven?
> This Jesus, who was taken up from you into heaven, will
> come in the same way as you saw him go into heaven.

Jesus came
with the intention of returning to heaven,
and shifting reality on earth.

And now
there is a human being
who is in heaven.

A man,
in the flesh
seated at the right hand of God.

And because the Trinity contains
a human being,
God can understand every aspect of human life.
He has experienced everything
in the human life
and he can relate.

He went low,
to the very depths of the human experience,
so that he could bring humanity
up to heaven with him.

And this leads to the next point:
Jesus is seated at the right hand of the Father.
That implies, as the Book of Hebrews notes,
that he is resting.
He is not a priest who daily offers sacrifices,
or makes an annual atonement.
He is seated,
because he is not a servant or a slave.
Jesus is the Sovereign.
And because he is resting,
he has become rest.
And we can live in him,
and rest in his rest.

He is seated,
and he rules and reigns.
And because of this,
we are seated with him.
As Paul says
in the first chapter of Ephesians,
Jesus Christ is seated above all
spiritual forces
and powers
and thought systems
in the universe.

In the next chapter he continues
and says that we too are seated with him
in the heavenly places.
In other words,
because of the presence of Christ in you,
you are seated above all
spiritual forces,
and powers,
and thought systems
in the universe.

Because of the humanity of Jesus,
we who are joined with him,
share in the benefits as members of his family.
We have heavenly genetics.

And because Jesus is seated with the Father,
he lives to pray for us.

And this heavenly intercession
is ongoing,
because he is outside time.
And we can align ourselves with his will.
And we can enter into the prayer of heaven
and heaven can pray through us.
And when we do not know how to pray,

heaven will
come to our aid
with groans too deep to understand.

Jesus promised that if he ascended
he would ask the Father
and the Father would send the Holy Spirit
to the earth.
Through the Holy Spirit,
we have the ability to experience the reality that
Paul describes in Colossians 1:27,
"Christ in you,
the hope of glory."
Everything that the Bible says
about the triumph of Jesus
through his
cross
and resurrection,
is now availabe to you,
because he has ascended into heaven.

We, in him,
are above all things.
We have made all captivity captive.
The life that raised him from the dead
is available to us.
The mind of Christ,
the wisdom,
the creative ability,
the emotional wellbeing,
and wholeness of God,
is available to us.

The fruit of the Holy Spirit:
love
joy
peace
patience

kindnesss
gentleness
and
self control
are available to us.

All because Jesus ascended to the Father.

And because Jesus ascended
to the right hand of God,
he said he would come again.
And when he does,
he will complete everything he began.

He ascended into heaven,
and is seated at the right hand of God,
the Father Almighty.

HE will COME AGAIN

We have come to the end of
the section about Jesus in the Creed.

The verb tense has moved from the past,
to the present,
and now,
the future.

The Christian story,
the story of the Kingdom,
is not over.

George Eldon Ladd,
in his *Theology of the New Testament*
describes where we are as "the already, but not yet Kingdom."

We are now somewhere in the middle.
And sometimes it feels
very muddled
and stuck.
Will this story ever end?
Will these problems ever get sorted out?
And if you read secular writers,
who are very aware of the problems in the world,
the future
is very
depressing.

I am going to tell you something shocking.
Human beings will never solve the world's problems.

Rather,
human beings will continue
to create more problems
as they make solutions without God.
God in his mercy
imparts wisdom and knowledge to us
as a grace to keep us going.

But as the anti-Christ spirit
increases in the earth,
that grace will become less and less.

The King is coming
to bring order.

Let's look at the two passages of Scripture
I quoted in the last chapter.

In the first chapter of Acts
we get an interesting description of the Ascension of Jesus.
Luke tells us that Jesus stepped into a cloud,
and when he was received into the cloud,
two men appeared and told the witnesses
that Jesus would return the same way.

Daniel Chapter 7
gives us a vision of this same event
from heaven's point of view.
In Daniel 7:13
we are given a description
of one like the Son of Man
who comes with the clouds of heaven
and this Son of Man
was given
dominion,
and glory,
and a kingdom,
that all people, nations, and languages
would serve him
and his dominion is an everlasting dominion,
and his Kingdom shall not be destroyed.
His kingdom will have no end.

Jesus Christ ascended to heaven
to receive everything,
so that he can return and bring it all with him.

And this Kingdom
the one he describes with stories and parables,
will be established in this earth.

So often people get obsessed
with strange details
about the second coming
and the fulfilling of prophecy,
but they miss "why."
Jesus isn't coming to blow up the earth.
He is coming to finally rule and reign on the earth.
His Kingdom is real,
not airy-fairy.

As we mentioned before,
in Hebrews it says that Jesus sat down.
He is no longer laboring,
because it is finished.

But some day,
Jesus is going to stand up.
And when he does
He is going back to work.

This time he is coming with a roar,
not a whimper.

And the Creed says
He is coming with glory.
"Glory" is an interesting word.
The word used in the original creed is "doxa."
This word comes to us today in the word "doxology"
"Glory be to the Father and to the Son, and to the Holy Spirit."

Doxa is the word that was used to translate
the Hebrew word "Kabod." (pronouced ka-BODE)
In the Bible,
Kabod is an important word.

It was the Kabod of the God
that rested in the tabernacle,
and it was the Kabod of God
that filled the temple and made it so no one could stand.
And it was the Kabod
that God let Moses encounter on the mountain.
And when it did,
Moses heard the Name of the LORD,
merciful,
and gracious,
and abundant in goodness in truth.
In Zechariah 2,
the Kabod of God will dwell in the midst of us
and form a wall of fire around us.

This word "glory"
in this sense means "weight."
It is full of gravitas--latin for weighty.
It is not just light,
it is Presence,
and Power.
It is substance.
And for those of us
who have had the great blessing to encounter it,
it is Holy.

So Jesus will come again,
and when he does
his very presence will win the argument.

The full dwelling of God,
in the flesh,
will dwell on earth in full manifestation.
And no one will be able to kill him
or stop the advance of his kingdom.

We have little glimpses in Scripture that indicate
the return of Jesus will be violent.

There are going to be people
who do not want a king like Jesus.

As it says in I Corinthians 15:22-26,

> For as in Adam all die, so also in Christ shall all be made
> alive. But each in his own order: Christ the first fruits,
> then at his coming those who belong to Christ.
> Then comes the end, when he delivers the kingdom to
> God the Father after destroying every rule and every
> authority and power. For he must reign until he has
> put all his enemies under his feet. The last enemy to be
> destroyed is death.

He must reign,
until he puts all his enemies under his feet.
He is going to return with his
glorious
weighty
Presence.

Charles Wesley described it this way.

> Lo! He comes with clouds descending,
> Once for favored sinners slain;
> Thousand thousand saints attending,
> Swell the triumph of His train:
> Hallelujah! Hallelujah!
> God appears on earth to reign!
>
> Every eye shall now behold Him
> Robed in dreadful majesty;
> Those who set at naught and sold Him,
> Pierced and nailed Him to the tree,
> Deeply wailing, deeply wailing,
> Shall the true Messiah see.

Every island, sea, and mountain,
Heav'n and earth, shall flee away;
All who hate Him must, confounded,
Hear the trump proclaim the day:
Come to judgment! Come to judgment!
Come to judgment! Come away!

Now redemption, long expected,
See in solemn pomp appear;
All His saints, by man rejected,
Now shall meet Him in the air.
Hallelujah! Hallelujah!
See the day of God appear!

Answer Thine own Bride and Spirit,
Hasten, Lord, the general doom!
The new Heav'n and earth t'inherit,
Take Thy pining exiles home:
All creation, all creation,
Travails! groans! and bids Thee come!

The dear tokens of His passion
Still His dazzling body bears;
Cause of endless exultation
To His ransomed worshippers;
With what rapture, with what rapture
Gaze we on those glorious scars!

Yea, Amen! let all adore Thee,
High on Thine eternal throne;
Savior, take the power and glory,
Claim the kingdom for Thine own!
O come quickly! O come quickly!
Everlasting God, come down!

And of course,
as Paul mentions,
the return of Jesus is the final act of the resurrection.

Jesus rose first,
but the day is coming
when all the dead in Christ shall rise.
And part of this rising
is meeting Jesus in the air.

But the point of this rising isn't the "rapture"
where the world descends into chaos
before Jesus burns it all up.

NO.
The point is
an indestructable army that can join with him
to rule and reign and bring order.
God's plan has always been a city
where we live in fellowship with him.

Intrinsically linked with the return of Jesus
is the last Judgement.
Jesus is returning to bring order,
not burn everything up.
Jesus is the Shalom-maker.
He is the Prince of Order.
And so,
he has to bring things into order.
And we need to never forget
Jesus is the Judge.

When we hear the word "judgement"
we think "punishment."

The biblical idea of judgement
is best described in Amos 7:7-8:
God puts a "plumb line" in the midst of Israel
and then identifies everything that is not "plumb."

God establishes the standard:
his word.

And then God asks us to stand up against this standard,
and see if we are off in some area.
This is God's judgement.

John's Gospel tells us that
the Father has given the Son
the job of judgement.

One of Satan's great lies is that there is a angry old man
with a long white beard
sitting in heaven with a gavel
anxious to judge you
and throw you in jail.

No.
Jesus
the God who became a man,
who was tempted in every way
as we are
will judge you.
The God who walked in your shoes
and felt the ultimate pain,
is the one who will decide
your eternal fate.

And Jesus is the Word.
He is the Plumb line.
He is the standard.

And Jesus says in John 12:47-48
that he will not judge those
who hear his words and receive him
but those who reject him
his words will be their own judgement.

In other words,
you can settle the day of judgement right now.
It is not something to keep you up at night.

Make Jesus Lord
and receive his word
and let it change you.
When you are in Jesus,
you are plumb.
It is those who reject him, the standard,
that will receive judgement against that standard.

As an aside,
many folks often see "11:11" on the clock.
Eleven is a transitional number,
and in the Bible
eleven is the number of judgement.
I have heard a lot of interpretations about this
phenomenon,
but the clearest and simplest is this:
we are in a time of judgement.

And clearly,
we live in a world that has an odd paradox.
Based on the the standard of history,
we live in one of the most morally depraved times.
And in the past when a society was morally bankrupt,
it was one society,
in one place.
And usually that society met a terrible end.

Today this moral bankruptcy appears to be in many places
across the world.
As the Book of Revelation ends,
the phrase "Behold, I am coming soon!"
is repeated several times.
Jesus is coming, and possibly very soon.

This is all about the Kingdom.
This Kingdom will never end.
And this Kingdom is a kingdom of life,
not a kingdom of death.

Jesus Christ is coming to rule and reign
and we who believe in him
and let his word come in and judge us
will participate in his dominion on the earth.
It is really good news.

His Kingdom will have no end.

And this is why the Creed does not end here,
but continues
in the Present tense
with the Person and work of the Holy Spirit.
God with us.
God in us.

we believe in the

HOLY
SPIRIT

We have now moved into the third portion of the Creed,
and once again we affirm "we believe."
We believe in the Holy Spirit.

We are in the present tense now.
We are not talking about doctrine or theology.
We are talking about experiencing God.
And the God we
interact with,
know,
and experience
is the Holy Spirit.

Jesus said, in John 6:63
that the Holy Spirit gives life,
and the works of humanity without the Holy Spirit
amount to nothing.

He echoes this again in John 15:5:
"apart from me you can do nothing."

The Holy Spirit
brooded over creation.
God breathed into Adam
the Holy Spirit and he lived.
And it was the Holy Spirit who was
grieved and left
at the Fall.
And death, not life, reigned in creation.

For believers who are accustomed
to hearing the voice of God,
seeing miracles,
and sensing the presence
of the Holy Spirit,
it is hard to fathom a world
where none of this
was possible.

In the Old Testament
this was not possible.
Here and there the Holy Spirit
would "come upon" someone
to prophesy,
do some heroic task,
or have revelation.

Before the New Covenant,
the Holy Spirit only visited people
to help them do a certain task.

And as I prepared this chapter
I did a search just to see if there were any brilliant
new talks or teachings on the Holy Spirit.
And I was reminded,
that many professing Christians
are still living in darkness,
believing that they have to do it all themselves
without God,
who call the Holy Spirit "it"
or a "thing,"
and don't even understand
the basics of the faith.

To many of them,
the Third Person of the Holy Trinity
is a vague ghost.

This is what Paul called in II Timothy
"a form of godliness with no power"
that for many in church
is normal.

Because they do not know God,
they have settled for religious activities
in place of relationship.

A relationship with God is risky and hard.
Religion is cheap and easy.

The primary purpose of the work of Christ
was to make the world safe for the Holy Spirit again.
It was the death and resurrection of Jesus
that opened the way for the Holy Spirit
back into creation.

John the Baptist said
that the Prophet
described by Moses in Deuteronomy 18
is the one on whom the Holy Spirit rests.
And Jesus,
when he came up from the water of Baptism
received the Holy Spirit.
It was in the Holy Spirit
that Jesus was able to
preach
teach,
work wonders,
and rise from the dead.
And he said his Kingdom would be marked by these signs.

And his title "Messiah" or Christ
means Anointed—with the Holy Spirit.
And those of us who are baptized into him
and born by water and the Holy Spirit
are called "Christians"
little anointed ones.
The same power that raised Jesus
from the dead,
is available to us.

The point of being a Christian
is not agreeing to a series
of doctrinal or philosophical points,
but rather,

to be born of the Holy Spirit
filled with the Holy Spirit,
and do greater works than Jesus did
through the Holy Spirit.

And so we move from doctrine
to experience.
The Holy Spirit is Emmanuel:
God with us.

Who is the Holy Spirit?
He is the Spirit who is Holy.
He is the Lord.
He is who he is.
He is the one who will be.
He is eternal.
He is all-powerful.
He is all-sufficient.
He is the Lord who is there—
when you get there you find he is there already.

Because the Holy Spirit is the presence of Jesus with us,
and is the Comforter,
and our Advocate—the one who fights for us—
people get chummy with the Holy Spirit.
This is very dangerous
because chumminess
can me mimicked
by our souls and emotions
and then the Holy Spirit is grieved and leaves.

We forget that the Holy Spirit
is also the Fear of the Lord.
We forget the Holy Spirit appeared
as earthquake, fire, and smoke
on Mount Sinai,
and then appeared as
fire and wind on the day of Pentecost.

You cannot call the Spirit of God
names we make up or
"Holy Spirit" as a proper name.
We do not tell the Holy Spirit what to do.
He is Holy.
You do not touch or get familiar
with A Holy One.

The Holy Spirit is mysterious.
The Holy Spirit was represented in the Tabernacle
by a seven branched candlestick covered with eyes.
The Book of Revelation tells us
there are Seven Spirits of God,
but the Holy Spirit is one.
From a symbolic point of the view
the Holy Spirit represents
completeness
wholeness
and fullness.

Jesus told the disciples to wait
until they received
the Promise of the Father
and the Power from on High.
And on the day of Pentecost
the Holy Spirit
who had left the temple at the time of Ezekiel
returned to the
New Covenant temples of the Holy Spirit--
human beings.

You,
not a building
not a statue
not a shrine
or a "thin place"
are the Temple of the Holy Spirit.

Your body is holy
and what you do in and with your body
reflects the Person who lives in you.

We believe
in the Presence of God with us.
The life of God is in us
through the Holy Spirit,
the Lord the Giver of Life.
This is the mystery of Christ in us.
Jesus Christ is living in you through
the Person of the Holy Spirit.
Those who do not know God
come up with
philosophical and theological explanations
to make sense of this.
And they all fall flat,
and they give you a Christianity
that doesn't work for you.

All of this is personal,
relational,
and experiential
by design.

Dr. Yonggi Cho had an extensive teaching
on how to experience daily prayer
in the temple of the Holy Spirit.
And in part of this prayer he used a phrase again and again:
"help me walk softly before you Lord,
that I may not grieve your Holy Spirit."
Help me walk softly.
Help me take the lowest place,
the quiet place
the submissive place.
Help me lay all my desires and beliefs before you
that I may be guided and directed by you,
because you will lead me into all truth.

We cannot know or experience life in the Holy Spirit
without constant yieldedness,
constant surrender,
constant submission.
And this kind of life will always look foolish.
As an old evangelist once said:
I am a fool for Christ,
Whose fool are you?

The Holy Spirit is described as a "dove"
in the baptism of Jesus.
When I was living in London,
I went to the park and fed pigeons.
And in the mix of pigeons was one white dove.
I am guessing it got loose after a wedding somewhere,
because they normally go back to their nest,
but this one was lost,
and so it hung out with the pigeons.

And this white dove would come
and sit with me on a park bench
in Sloane Square.
Unlike the pigeons,
he was not aggressive.
He was very gentle,
and a bit skittish.
Any quick movement or loud noise
would make him fly away.
But if I was quiet,
and calm
he would come close
and sit next to me,
sometimes for almost an hour at a time.
I got him to eat out of my hand.

When people ask me about listening to God
I always say the same thing.
First you have to get quiet.

You have to sit,
and settle down
and then you will begin to hear God speak.

And I believe it is important to "prime the pump"
with the Words of the Holy Spirit,
recorded for us in the Bible.
You see,
the Holy Spirit is the one who speaks in Scripture.
It is the voice of the Holy Spirit that we read
through the Prophets.

Many spiritual people think they can move beyond Scripture
and receive revelation that surpasses this.
There is no difference between
liberal theology,
charismatic theology that is weird,
errors that have crept into the historic churches,
and false cults.
They all believe
that they don't have to be corrected
by the Bible.
And this grieves the Holy Spirit.
This is why all these things
become dead monoliths.
It is the Holy Spirit
who is the Inspiration.
And right there,
Inspiration is the word
"breathing."
And the Holy Spirit in Hebrew
is the "Ruach haKodesh."
The Breath that is Holy.

The Holy Spirit
is always in the creation
of new things.

It was the Holy Spirit who filled
Bezalel
and he received the same revelation that Moses received,
and was able to construct the Tabernacle.

The Holy Spirit
is the force
and ability
of Creation.

Anywhere where there is no life,
there is no Holy Spirit.
And this is why we need to walk softly,
because our human souls can mimic
the Holy Spirit for a while.
We can easily get off track
and think our human thoughts and feelings
are the Spirit of God.
This is why we need to
constantly humble ourselves
go low,
and submit to Scripture.
When we submit to Scripture,
we are submitting to the Author of Scripture.

I was at a party recently
and some friends were talking about
"how can they get
the Holy Spirit
moving again at their church."

I just listened.
A few years ago I was staying
in a bed and breakfast in England,
and an old colleague in ministry
was staying there as well.
Over breakfast he commented
"that we are in between renewals."

Your experience of the Holy Spirit
can be continuous
and ongoing.
The Holy Spirit
loves broken and contrite hearts.
The Holy Spirit loves when we make His word
our home.
The Holy Spirit loves
when we offer ourselves as worship.
Paul tells us in Romans 12:2
that spiritual worship is
offering our bodies as living sacrifices.
And in doing this
we are transformed
by the renewing of our minds.
The Holy Spirit renews our minds
and transforms us.
And this is worship.
And this is renewal.
And this is awakening.
This is how we worship and glorify the Holy Spirit,
by yielding and saying "yes."
By living in his word.
By coming under the Lordship of Jesus.

And out of this,
the Holy Spirit gives life.
And that life is manifested in three things:
Fruit,
Gifts,
and Offices.

Jesus said to judge a tree by its fruit.
And when we eat of the
Tree of the Holy Spirit
we will produce
Love, joy, peace, patience, kindness,
goodness, gentleness, and self-control.

When we manifest this fruit in difficult situations,
people stand up and notice.

When we choose to walk
in something other than the Holy Spirit,
we manifest other fruit:
adultery,
sexual immorality,
perversion,
greed,
idolatry,
witchcraft,
hatred,
false teaching,
envy,
strife,
sedition and rebellion,
sectarianism and political factions,
addiction
orgies and debauched living.

I have lived through several "moves" of the Holy Spirit,
and this week I was pondering
some of the history I have seen.
I noticed the pattern that the same leaders
who attacked the charismatic renewal
we now know were covering up
all kinds of sexual immorality.
Religion is deadly.
These truths in Scripture are true.
You will always know a tree by its fruit.

The gifts of the Holy Spirit
make it possible
to display
the power and presence of God
in difficult situations,
and to help us.

These are abilities beyond us:
Tongues,
healing,
miracles,
faith,
knowledge,
prophecy,
and many more.
The gifts enable us
to do more than we could do
in our own strength and ability.
These gifts allow us
to advance the Kingdom in a supernatural war.

And finally,
the offices,
Apostle,
Prophet,
Evangelist,
Pastor,
and Teacher.
These exist to build up
the Body of Christ into maturity
and build the people of God into a living temple.

Many people think
that the Holy Spirit
is always about freedom and liberty.
And true,
where the Spirit of the Lord is, there is freedom.
But living for chaos is not the Holy Spirit,
and this is where some of our friends get in trouble.

This is the Spirit of Shalom—
the presence of order.
This is the God who created all things.
Creation is not chaos.
We have to surrender to order in the Holy Spirit.

We have to yield
and follow his direction.
We have to say "yes" and go where he asks us.
And we have to have soft and malleable hearts.

The Holy Spirit is the Life of God with us.
The Holy Spirit is the Life of God through us.
And the Holy Spirit is the Life of God in us.

Come Holy Spirit,
fill the hearts of your faithful people
and kindle in us,
the Fire of your love.

We believe in the Holy Spirit,
the Lord, the Giver of Life,
who proceeds from the Father and the Son.
With the Father and the Son,
He is worshipped and glorified.
He has spoken through the Prophets.

we believe in the CHURCH

Over this journey through the Nicene Creed,
we have encountered a handful of surprises along the way.

Each section of the Creed begins with
We Believe:
We believe in the Father
We believe in the Son
We believe in the Holy Spirit
We believe in the Church.

Wait!
What?
We believe in the church?

If what Jesus
and the New Testament said is true:
I am in you and you are in me.
I am in the Father and the Father is in me.
Apart from me you can do nothing.
Receive the Holy Spirit.
Do not leave the city until you receive Power from on High.
In him we live and move and have our being.
We are his body and he is the head.
We are seated with him in heavenly places
above all rule and authority.

Then,
the church is the visible
tangible expression
of God
in the earth
until Jesus returns.

Of course,
for many people,
including most Protestants,
this is a problem.

As Martin Luther once said,
"The Church is my mother,
and she is a whore."
And if you read the newspapers
you might also think
the church is an abusive spouse,
or an organized crime syndicate.

We hear this word "church" and
we hear "buildings and institutions."
And these institutions,
in our day,
probably at a level
not seen since the Protestant Reformation,
are hopelessly corrupt.
At least that's the way it seems.

One of the Professors I worked for at Asbury,
Don Boyd,
once said that
the primary argument
for the existence of God
is the continuing existence on earth
of the church.
Because no institution could exist for 2000 years
the way the church operates.
And this is true.

The word in the New Testament
and in the Creed
that is translated "Church"
is "Ekklesia."
It has come down to us in the word "ecclesiastic"
meaning "of the church."

And the Ekklesia
is not
a building or an institution.

In Ancient Greece
when there was a difficult situation
that needed a decision
and action by the whole community,
a town cryer would go through the streets
and shout the news
and gather an assembly.
The called ones
would deliberate
 and make governmental decisions
in the face of calamity and crisis.
This gathering of "called out ones"
was called the ekklesia.

Although there are other words
in the New Testament
for gatherings and congregations,
Jesus chose this one
"a gathering of called ones
with governmental authority"
for his community.

This was different than the synagogue:
a congregation of at least 10 Jewish men,
or koinonia,
a gathering for fellowship and comaraderie.
It was a gathering with a purpose
with authority,
and with power
to establish the Kingdom in the earth.

And separated from the Kingdom,
the human church becomes a monster,
and generally becomes at odds
with what God is doing.

This is why John Wesley said
that the church must be in a state of constant reformation.

Whenever the church
becomes self-satisfied
with the status quo,
embraces religious pride,
and the traditions of men
then history has shown
that there needs to be a great correction.

This happened at the turn of the first millenium
and it happened 500 years ago,
and it is happening now.

But the Ekklesia is eternal,
and it will continue,
regardless of what will happen to the human institutions.

The Ekklesia is one.
The Church is One Body
to quote Paul.
And Jesus Christ
is the Head of the Church.
Regardless of what it says
over the door of the building,
all baptized believers belong to one entity.
This is about birth into Christ,
a new nation
a royal priesthood,
and a called out people (an ekklesia).

The Ekklesia
does not replace Israel,
but rather fulfills Israel.
The Ekklesia acts
as God's representation on earth
with his spiritual authority
to exercise
and continue
his dominion.

As it says in the seventh chapter of Revelation,
we are called to be a kingdom of priests
who will serve our God
and reign on the earth.

Back during the days
of the Charismatic renewal
we would have prayer meetings
with catholics and all kinds of protestants,
and we all talked the same language
and did the same things.
It was the Holy Spirit that made us one.
We were one in the spirit.
And all the denominational institutions
hated this, and eventually stepped in and killed it.
And then they called meetings about Christian unity.
There is a lesson there.

But this unseen Body cannot be divided,
it is one.

And because it is the Body of Christ
it is Holy.
It is set apart.
It is the Temple of the Holy Spirit,
and when we are walking in the Spirit,
we bear the fruit of the Spirit,
and we reflect the holiness of the Head.

And this holiness is not about religion.
It is about being bought by the blood of Christ,
and holiness gives us the fear of God.
We do not speak about members of this body
in unholy ways,
because this body is holy,
and they are part of this body.
And we do not touch or get familiar with the holy.
Familiarity breeds contempt.

Intimacy is precious.
Intimacy with God
is not so you can build a ministry,
a church,
or raise money.
That is prostitution,
and that leads us back to Luther's quote.
And we are in a time again
where the church has gone a-whoring,
trying to make as much money as possible.
This is not holy.

Holiness fills us with a fear of the Lord.
We are not in charge of the Church,
we must walk softly before the Lord at all times.

This holiness comes from the waters of the Baptism,
from the Presence and Anointing of the Holy Spirit,
and the coming to share in the Body and Blood of Christ.
All these things make us holy,
and the inward transformation
results in holy living.
God works from the inside out
not the outside in.

And interestingly,
all these things make us one with Christ
and one with each other.

The Church is also "catholic."
Now this word
is the one that makes many people bristle.
There is a great video version
of the creed that I found,
but have chosen not to use
because they replaced the word "catholic"
with Christian.
They are not the same word.

All blessings in Hebrew begin this way:
"Baruch atta Adonai, elohainu malech Ha Olam."
Blessed are you Lord our God,
King of the Universe.

"Ha Olam" is the Universe.
But it is not just outer space.
It is all time.
All places.
All dimensions.
All spiritual realms.
All in all.
God is the King over all and in all.
And the Greek translation of this concept is "Katholikon."

The called out Body,
is the only Body of Christ
in all times,
in all places,
and throughout all dimensions,
seen and unseen.
There is only one church,
and that church is undivided
by life or death,
by religious authorities,
by physical boundaries.
Why?
Because Jesus Christ,
through the Holy Spirit,
forms a mystical body
that is more real than the bodies we see.

C.S. Lewis,
in the book *The Screwtape Letters*,
records the letters between
an elder demon
and a younger one
on how to tempt and destroy a Christian.

This quote,
on the demonic view of the Church,
is very insightful.

> One of our great allies at present is the Church itself. Do
> not misunderstand me. I do not mean the Church as we
> see her spread out through all time and space and root-
> ed in eternity, terrible as an army with banners. That,
> I confess, is a spectacle which makes even our boldest
> tempters uneasy. But fortunately it is quite invisible to
> these humans.

The church described here
is what is meant by "Catholic."

It has been said that
"there is no salvation outside the church."
The person who said this
was talking about their denomination,
but it is a true saying.
Outside the Body of Christ
there is no salvation.
There is only one way to God
through the Lord Jesus Christ,
and any body or organization not connected
to his mystical body
will lead you to the path of destruction.

"Apostolic "is linked to Catholic,
and this is extremely important:
The "mystical catholic church"
is never separate from the
faith and practice
given to us from the hands of the Apostles.

In other words,
Jesus taught his disciples
the true and only way to God.

That way was then taught
to succeeding generations.

My roots are in an Apostolic tradition.
The church that raised me claimed
"Apostolic Succession."
What that means in a perfect world is this:
the current authority
through time
was passed from one father to son
by the laying on of hands
all the way back to the Apostles,
and for many western Christians,
that means Peter.

Sadly, we do not live in a perfect world.
That model has been used and abused throughout history.

The church I once served
is no longer Apostolic,
because it no longer teaches the apostolic faith,
the faith that the Apostles gave us.
You cannot have one without the other.
And the true church teaches that
Jesus Christ came in the flesh,
was born of the Virgin Mary by the Holy Spirit,
Died on the Cross for all humanity,
Was raised from the dead on the third day by the Holy Spirit,
Ascended into heaven and is seated above all rule and authority,
and
will come again to judge the living and the dead.
And to be part of this church
you must confess with your mouth
Jesus Christ is Lord,
and believe in your heart
that God raised him from the dead.
And by faith in him
you will be saved.

Anything less than that
is not catholic,
not apostolic,
and not the Ekklesia.

The Holy Spirit is not limited
by human rules and traditions
but rather is looking for those
who proclaim the Apostolic witness.
Jesus is always happy to jump the fence
because whoever is not against him is for him.

And we are back to holy.
This is holy.
Our faith is holy.
It is for all times in all places in all dimensions.
It is spiritual reality.
It is this one,
eternal,
undivided,
community,
that has continued to stand
through persecutions,
through empires,
through wars and rumours of wars,
through error and false teaching,
through heresy and schism,
through scandals and calamities,
and through all the chances and changes of this fleeting life.

At its best the Church has been salt and light.
She has created written languages,
preserved the wisdom of even her enemies
in monasteries when civilization collapsed,
founded hospitals and schools,
ended slavery time and again,
reformed countries and nations,
invented solutions and solved problems,

restored broken civilizations,
and raise the multitudes up to life.
She has been there when grandma died,
stood by when someone needed to talk,
prayed for leaders when they needed guidance,
and fed those who needed bread.
She is the spouse for whom Jesus died,
who will one day come before him as a spotless bride.
Redeemed from her whoredom to virginity.

The Church is much bigger
than a group of people
gathering someplace
who all like each other
and who all agree about some fine point of doctrine
or delight in some refined religious rites.

No.
This is a sad and inadequate counterfeit.

The Church is the seen
and unseen communion
of all those who have heard
the voice of the Shepherd
and who have come out of darkness
and been washed in his marvelous light.
We have been buried with him in baptism
and seated with him at the fellowship of his table.
We look forward to an endless celebration there.

We believe in one, holy,
catholic and apostolic Church.

ONE BAPTISM

The Day of Pentecost began with fire,
and ended with water.
Luke tells us in Acts,
that 3000 people were baptized that day.

The last few lines of the Creed
are the practical expressions
of our belief in the Holy Spirit.

Our faith in Jesus
brings us into fellowship
with the Holy Spirit,
and forms a spiritual body,
the church.
And you enter into that body through birth—
by water and the Holy Spirit.
The only way into
the Body of Christ
is to be born into it.

This line in the Creed
"We acknowledge one baptism for the remission of sins"
is the most Scriptural of all,
and it has its foundation
in the very beginning of the Church.
This is from the last line
of Peter's sermon on the Day of Pentecost.

"Repent and be baptized
every one of you
in the name of Jesus Christ
for the remission of sins,
and you shall receive the gift
of the Holy Ghost." (Acts 2:38-39)

Let's unpack this a bit,
because it is perfect baptismal theology.

Repent.
That is,
turn from your sin to God.

"Repentance" in the New Testament is "metanoia."
Metanoia means
to be transformed in your thinking.
In the Old Testament,
the word is "shuv."
To turn from your sin to God.
The turning is to a person—Jesus.

(In my book *Body: Where You Belong*
I take two chapters to explain this fully.)

Here Peter says,
"Turn from your sin,
change your thinking,
and come into Jesus—
and then you will receive Power from the Holy Ghost
to live a different kind of life—in Jesus."

When you are baptized,
it is an outward sign
that in Jesus you are no longer a sinner:
you have a new identity
from sinner to a holy one.
And the Holy Spirit confirms that you are in him
and the power of God comes to you to change you.
All of this is from the inside out.

This is why Peter does not say you have to take a class
or do a bunch of things to be baptized.
You have to turn from your sin
and in the turning
the Holy Spirit will agree with your decision
and give you power to keep turning.

God is the one working and acting in baptism.
Not us.

Although fire is very apparent on the Day of Pentecost,
water
is the primary symbol
of the Holy Spirit in Scripture.

The Holy Spirit brooded
over the waters of creation.
When Bezalel was filled,
the Hebrew indicates
something like the movement of water.
Jesus said out of your belly
will flow rivers of living water.
Jesus is baptized and receives
the Holy Spirit as he comes out of the water.

And in John's gospel,
there is a sub-plot that tells another story,
if you follow the water.
And that plot climaxes at the end of the book,
when Peter jumps into the water,
comes up,
and is commissioned by Jesus.
John is telling the story of the Day of Pentecost
through the metaphor of water.
The water in John is the Holy Spirit.

Jesus said,
in John 3,
that no one can come into the Kingdom
unless they are born by water and the Holy Spirit.
From the perspective of Jesus and the New Testament
Baptism
is the New Birth.

In the New Testament mind
doing,
not thinking or agreeing,
is believing.

You are saved when
you are born by water and the Holy Spirit,
and Jesus said,
that when you are born this way,
you are born from above.
It is not just you making a decision,
there is a transaction
and you are welcomed
into the Name of Jesus

In this sense, the Name of Jesus
is the new Kingdom
like the name of Israel
is the Jewish people.
You are now part of that invisible company
the Ekklesia,
the called out ones
the governing body
of the Kingdom on earth.

This is in fulfillment of the prophesy in Ezekiel 36:22-27,

> Therefore, give the people of Israel this message from
> the Sovereign Lord:
> I am bringing you back, but not because you deserve it.
> I am doing it to protect my holy name,
> on which you brought shame while you were scattered
> among the nations. I will show how holy my great name
> is—the name on which you brought shame among the
> nations.
>
> And when I reveal my holiness through you
> before their very eyes,

says the Sovereign Lord,
then the nations will know that I am the Lord.
For I will gather you up from all the nations and bring
you home again to your land.

Then I will sprinkle clean water on you,
and you will be clean.
Your filth will be washed away,
and you will no longer worship idols.

And I will give you a new heart,
and I will put a new spirit in you.
I will take out your stony, stubborn heart
and give you a tender, responsive heart.
And I will put my Spirit in you
so that you will follow my decrees
and be careful to obey my regulations.

First,
it says God will reveal his holiness through you.
The King James says
"I will be sanctified in you."
When God reveals his holiness in them,
the nations will see it and believe.
And God will sprinkle clean water on them
and put a new spirit in them
and they will be clean.
God will put his law in them
from the inside out.

So, on the Day of Pentecost,
we see an echo
of the first Pentecost,
when Moses received the law on Mount Sinai.
With fire and wind and mysterious voices
Moses received the commandments.

And on the day of Pentecost in Jerusalem
the fire and wind came again
and this time
the believers were filled with the Holy Spirit.
They began to experience
what Paul describes in Romans 8:1,
"There is therefore now no condemnation
for the law of the Spirit of life in Christ Jesus
has set me free from the law of Sin and death."

When we are baptized
into the Name of Jesus
as Jesus instructed us,
in the Name of the Father, the Son, and the Holy Spirit,
we are brought under a new law
and we are citizens in a new country,
a new Kingdom.

This is not a ritual that
shows you made a personal decision,
and then you are left to follow new laws and
spend your life in effort to try to be a good person.
As we all know,
and have seen in so many lives around us,
this only leads to failure.
When you are brought into the Kingdom
through the water of Baptism
the Holy Spirit comes in
and you are to be like Peter—jumping in.
And then the law of the Kingdom
begins to manifest in your life.

And this is why
there is only one baptism.
As Paul said--
There is one body,
One Spirit,
even as ye are called into one hope of your calling,

One Lord
one faith,
one baptism,
One God and Father of all,
who is above all, and through all,
and in you all.
(Ephesians 4:4-6)

As I mentioned,
there is only one church,
and the only way in is through Baptism.
And this is why we resist rebaptizing people.
Doing this is like someone
going through the citizenship process
and becoming a citizen.
And then a few years later,
deciding they want to become citizens again,
because the first one didn't count.

Baptism is not about you or your experience.
It is about coming into the covenant.
There is only one Baptism.

When you are in him,
you belong to him.
And when you belong to him
you come back to him
every time you share in the Body and Blood of Christ.
The door in is through water.
And the sign you are in is sharing at the table.
It is very simple.

There is only one Baptism,
because there is only one Holy Spirit.
The Holy Spirit is the one acting here,
giving birth through water,
just like the creation in the beginning.

And as Paul says in 2 Corinthians 5:17:
if anyone is in Christ,
that person is a new creation.

As Jesus said to Nicodemus,
you must be born again.
You must have a second birth by the Holy Spirit
and become a spiritual being.

In our community,
we renew our Baptismal promises
several times a year.
This is the form we use,
and I encourage you to use it too.

And so I ask you:
Do you renounce Satan?
I do.
And all his works?
I do.
And all his empty show?
I do.
Do you renounce sin,
so as to live in the freedom of the children of God?
I do.
Do you renounce the glamour of evil,
so that sin may have no mastery over you?
I do.
Do you receive the Lord Jesus Christ?
I do.

Do you believe in God, the Father Almighty,
Creator of heaven and earth?
I do.

Do you believe in Jesus Christ, his only Son,
our Lord, who was conceived by the Holy Spirit,
who was born of the Virgin Mary,

suffered death and was buried,
rose again from the dead
and is seated at the right hand of the Father?
I do.

Do you believe in the Holy Spirit,
the holy Catholic Church,
the communion of saints,
the forgiveness of sins,
the resurrection of the body,
and life everlasting?
I do.

May almighty God,
the Father of our Lord Jesus Christ,
who has given us new birth
by water and the Holy Spirit
and bestowed on us forgiveness of our sins,
keep us by his grace,
in Christ Jesus our Lord, for eternal life.
Amen.

the LIFE of the world to come

The Creed doesn't end with an ending.
It ends with anticipation.

We look forward to the Resurrection of the Dead
and the life of the world to come.

There is more.
This life is not all there is.
The God of the Bible
of the Creed
is the Lord of Life.
Life.
Creation.
Fullness.
Multiplication.

This God created life.
God created human beings to be full of life.
God created humanity to increase and multiply,
to fill the earth with order
and create a city
for God and humankind
to relate to one another
without a barrier.
No temple, no ritual, no intermediaries.
A direct relationship of love.
And this promise
began when Jesus
walked out of the tomb with a Resurrection body.
He was a living temple,
and then at Pentecost,
human beings became the temples of the Holy Spirit.
We are now holy beings.
And this human body is holy.

Dietrich Bonhoeffer in his pastor's manual *Spiritual Care*
notes that when missionaries went into Europe
the practice of cremation of the dead ceased.

With their mission,
the practice of Christian burial began.
Christians,
because of the resurrection of the dead
honored the body.
The body is a holy thing.

And the promise that we look forward to
is the day when our spirits, souls, and bodies are reunited.
And this resurrection that we experience
is a continuation of the Resurrection of Jesus.
What we practice symbolically in our Christian lives
will one day be expressed in a living reality.

As Paul says in I Corinthians 15:20-25

> But in fact Christ has been raised from the dead, the first
> fruits of those who have fallen asleep. For as by a man
> came death, by a man has come also the resurrection of
> the dead. For as in Adam all die, so also in Christ shall all
> be made alive. But each in his own order: Christ the first
> fruits, then at his coming those who belong to Christ.
> Then comes the end, when he delivers the kingdom to
> God the Father after destroying every rule and every
> authority and power. For he must reign until he has
> put all his enemies under his feet. The last enemy to be
> destroyed is death.

Jesus will come back
to rule and reign on the earth,
and some will experience extended life,
and others will at some point be raised from the dead.

Jesus is returning,
with a glorified host of holy human beings
and their job will be to destroy
every ruler,
authority,

and power
that refuses to submit
to the King and his Kingdom.
And this resurrection
will be the beginning
of a new heaven and a new earth.
This is the beginning of eternal life—
life without time
and without end.

Paul continues in I Corinthians 15:50-53:

> I tell you this, brethren: flesh and blood cannot inherit
> the kingdom of God, nor does the perishable inherit the
> imperishable.
>
> Lo! I tell you a mystery. We shall not all sleep, but we
> shall all be changed, in a moment, in the twinkling of
> an eye, at the last trumpet. For the trumpet will sound,
> and the dead will be raised imperishable, and we shall
> be changed. For this perishable nature must put on the
> imperishable, and this mortal nature must put on im-
> mortality.

This is all about the Kingdom.
Jesus began a Kingdom that will never end
and these bodies of ours
cannot live eternally.

God began a new thing in Jesus
a new kind of creation—
a body that cannot decay,
that can pass through
space and time and physical limitations.
And that new creation,
not part of the fallen one,
is not subject to death.

You will live forever in a physical body,
with Jesus and the rest of the Body of Christ.

One of the great tragedies
in the Christian faith
is the influence of Greek philosophy
and pagan ideas on the Body of Christ.
Angels, from what I see in Scripture,
do not look like women in pink dresses with wings.

They are all masculine beings
all of them are powerful
and quite a few are scary.

The spiritual realm
is not a whispy, gauzy, ethereal thing.
It is not like you see in the movies and in the cartoons.
As C.S. Lewis rightly portrayed
in the book *The Great Divorce*
it is much more real than our realm.
In that book he describes
blades of grass that will cut through our feet.
The spiritual realm is more real than this one.
The color there is more vivid than the color here.
Mass is more solid and beyond our understanding.
The spiritual realm is not a shadow of this one,
and Christian souls do not become shades after death.
Our future and our hope is not to become a ghost.

And for many of us,
heaven is not the realm of the *New Yorker* cartoon
where George and Ethel
are sitting in easy chairs on a cloud
watching television
in costumes left over from the church Nativity play.
You are not going to become
a play angel on a cloud forever.

No.
The plan is for you to go outside time forever,
and continue
what you began here.
The life after this one
is more than the one here.
What was sown in weakness
will be raised again in strength
and you will continue to be who you are.
You will not be something else,
and this life will not be wasted or discarded.

Imagine a life
where every day
is better than
the day before.

Imagine a life where every day is another day
to improve
to create
to express
to be strengthened
to grow
and to increase.
Where you become more and more you.

The real you,
not a fake you,
not a you that hides and protects.
A you where you become more and more glorious,
more and more all the best bits of who you are.

You are designed to be an eternal being.
On this side
we discover and walk in the fact that
we have eternal needs.
And on that side we will discover
that the needs are all met.

We will keep
increasing,
and growing,
and fulfilling all our dreams and destinies.

This is just a shadow of that.

> And I saw no temple in the city, for its temple is the
> Lord God the Almighty and the Lamb. And the city has
> no need of sun or moon to shine upon it, for the glory
> of God is its light, and its lamp is the Lamb. By its light
> shall the nations walk; and the kings of the earth shall
> bring their glory into it, and its gates shall never be shut
> by day—and there shall be no night there; they shall
> bring into it the glory and the honor of the nations. But
> nothing unclean shall enter it, nor any one who practices
> abomination or falsehood, but only those who are writ-
> ten in the Lamb's book of life. (Revelation 21:22-26)

> There shall no more be anything accursed, but the
> throne of God and of the Lamb shall be in it, and his
> servants shall worship him; they shall see his face, and
> his name shall be on their foreheads. And night shall be
> no more; they need no light of lamp or sun, for the Lord
> God will be their light, and they shall reign for ever and
> ever. (Revelation 22:3-5)

There is more.
There is more.
There is more.

As we end this journey,
I encourage you
to keep going.

Keep pursuing
and growing in all that God has for you.

Keep walking close to Jesus
and keep getting healed
and becoming whole.

When painful things
and painful seasons arise,
don't settle
keep growing.

Let the stony bits of your heart go
and let the Lord give you bits of a heart of flesh.
Forgive and be forgiven.
Love one another
and do unto others
as you would have them do unto you.

It will be worth it.
It will be worth it.

The very best is yet to come.

Works Cited

Benedict. Pope, and Vittorio Messori. *The Ratzinger Report: An Exclusive Interview on the State of the Church.* San Francisco: Ignatius Press, 1985.

Ladd, George Eldon, and Donald Alfred Hagner. *A Theology of the New Testament.* Grand Rapids (MI): Eerdmans, 2002.

Lewis, C. S. *The Screwtape Letters.* 2009.

Acknowledgements

Special thanks
to my friend Dr. Steve Seamands
Professor Emeritus of Theology at
Asbury Theological Seminary
who has been a mentor for nearly 30 years.

I am grateful for the edits and corrections
that Andrea Van Boven and Glenda Gibson
shared after initial publication.
Your help brought this book closer to
excellence. Thank you.

This book would
not have happened
without Beth Charashim,
the Belonging House Fellowship
Sunday congregation.
Your thoughts,
feedback,
and questions
were invaluable.

I am grateful to our growing
army of artists around the world.
You keep making me
answer the questions
people really are asking.

CHRIST JOHN OTTO
earned a B.S. in Christian Education
and Bible from Houghton College
and an M.Div.
from Asbury Theological Seminary.

He is the founder of
Belonging House,
an international fellowship of
artists and creative people.

Since 2006 he has sent an email to artists and
creative people. You can find out more at
Belonging.House.